Gimmies, Bogeys and Business

GIMMIES, BOGEYS AND BUSINESS:

An Insider's Guide On How To Use Golf For Professional Success

Jane Blalock
Dawn-Marie Driscoll

John Caldwell's cartoons
selected by Michelle Urry

MasterMedia Limited
New York

Published by MasterMedia Limited.

Library of Congress Cataloging-in-Publication Data

Blalock, Jane/Driscoll, Dawn-Marie.

"Gimmies, Bogeys And Business: An Insider's Guide On How To Use Golf
For Professional Success"/Jane Blalock, Dawn-Marie Driscoll

ISBN 1-5710-060-2

Designed by Jennifer McNamara
Printed in the United States of America
Production services by Graafiset International, Baldwin, N.Y.

10 9 8 7 6 5 4 3 2 1

Contents

FOREWORD

Golf and business go hand in hand. But it also is great fun for the family and an adventurous sport for people of all ages. Too, it is a sport where one does not need to find an opponent—it can be enjoyed solo.

My initial purpose in learning to play golf was to entertain clients and, believe me, I did. Even as a five-year veteran of the sport, my game can still be entertaining! The only title I've ever won is "Countess Hit The Rock." But I really do love to play. I also want my children to play so they can enjoy golf all their lives.

As I reflect on my yet brief but enduring passion for the game, I believe the two most important goals are to find a good instructor to teach the basics for whatever skill level you wish to aspire to, and to understand the rules of the game—both on and off the course. Reading this his book will help you achieve both.

Executives are turning golf into a whole new game—understanding that the sport may be their most effective tool in today's competitive market. But private lessons and a few weekends watching ESPN or the Golf Channel aren't enough to give new golfers the social skills they need to combine work and leisure. There are more opportunities for embarrassment than there are to lose balls. The only difference is that you know with certainty when your ball is lost but you might not know when you've committed a faux pas, and your golf companion might not reveal it.

Business golf is different than tournament golf. If you are going to use golf for business, you want to use it correctly. *Gimmies, Bogeys And Business* can show you how.

—Diana Graham, President, STRATCO Inc.

PREFACE

Golf is just another sport for Jane Blalock, a natural athlete who played basketball, baseball and bowled as a child. But unlike golfing greats such as Tiger Woods, who started playing when he was two, Jane picked up her first set of golf clubs when she was 13 when she played in a club tournament with her mother in New Hampshire.

Jane came from an athletic family—although her father was a more avid sports fan than player. But Jane was always encouraged to be as active as her brothers Jack and Jim, and thrived on physical activity and competition. She took to golf easily and won her first trophy at age 13 in a 9-hole event for girls in Concord, N.H. By the time she was 17 she was shooting in the mid-80s, beating such talented golfers as noted skier Suzy Chaffee, and winning four consecutive New England junior championships.

When it came time to go to college, Jane headed off to Rollins College in Florida where she could play golf year round, as well as a variety of other sports while working toward a degree in history. Her return home to New England in 1967 was short-lived, and she soon headed back to Florida to study golf with Bob Toski at the Ocean Reef Club in Key Largo.

As Toski changed almost every aspect of her game, Jane lived at the club, cleaned clubs, picked up range balls and did odd jobs to continue her lessons.

In January of 1969 Jane entered the Burdine's Invitational, a tour event in Miami. Her goal was to play big-time amateur golf and make the U.S. team for the Curtis Cup. Much to her surprise, she finished fifth and decided to turn pro. In her first year as a professional she was honored as "Rookie of the Year."

That was the start of an astounding career for a very competitive golfer. In 18 years on the Ladies Professional Golf Association Tour, Jane won 29 LPGA Titles, two Triple Crown Titles and three World Ladies Championships in Japan. The seventh professional woman golfer to achieve the million-dollar mark in earnings, Jane still holds the record of playing in 299 tournaments without missing a cut—from 1969 to her last event in 1980.

Jane is straightforward about what it takes to compile a winning record. Sure, she wore a lucky pair of shorts, ate tuna fish for breakfast and had the support of good teachers and loyal friends on the tour. But in retrospect, her advice is as applicable to those trying to succeed in business as on the course—"Recognize when you have opportunities and then execute."

Jane is still looking for opportunities and executing with excellence.

In 1990 Jane launched the Jane Blalock Company, which has since earned national recogintion as one of the premier sports marketing firms. Her company specializes in developing golf, ski and tennis tournaments and special events for companies and organizations.

The company was inspired by Jane's dissatisfaction with the way many golf events were being run. After she retired from the tour, Jane played in many corporate golf events and would cringe when she'd watch how disorganized they were.

"I knew the sponsors weren't getting the most out of the event," she says. "The participants weren't benefitting either because they didn't know how effective a golf event could be. So I started with one or two clients and helped run events as well as plan them. Now we handle everything from A-to-Z, including transportation."

Jane's staff of former world-class athletes and marketing professionals now produces events all over the country, from the Gillette LPGA Golf Clinics for Women to the Volvo Legends Series. But the most requested golf lesson is the pre-cocktail hour, off-the-record "etiquette seminar."

"I don't think there's a question I haven't heard from business golfers," Jane says, "and it tells me two things. First, there are many new golfers who understand that this is a game of tradition, rules and courtesy. They may know how to play but they also want to know how to act.

"But more important, these golfers—and the advertisers who are trying to reach them—understand that golf and business go hand in hand. Though golf is not inexpensive to play, the economic returns can be great. I didn't fully appreciate this while I was out there on the tour. Sure, I wanted to win, but in one sense I couldn't see the forest through the trees. Now that I have stepped back, I can see the increasing popularity of golf, particularly among businesspeople. And I understand why—they are as passionate about the game as I am."

While Jane Blalock was a youngster playing golf in New Hampshire, Dawn-Marie Driscoll was attending summer camp in Massachusetts, doing everything but playing golf—swimming, sailing, tennis, canoeing. In college and law school she was a social athlete only.

Then came several decades as a corporate lawyer. As Vice President of Corporate Affairs and General Counsel of Filene's, a Boston-based department store chain, she approved the checks to help support charity golf events, but never attended any. The pace of her crisis-filled retailing environment was too hectic to take up a new sport.

Later, as a partner in the law firm of Palmer & Dodge, her rationale for ignoring the sport was the same. It continued when she became director of several mutual funds and private companies, and even when she became the head of her own consulting firm. "Driving" was how you got to a business meeting. "Chip" was what you served with salsa. "Birdie" was what perched in her Florida back yard.

But golf entered Dawn-Marie's radar screen in an unexpected manner. In 1990 she was invited to be a visitor-in-residence at The Bunting Institute at Radcliffe College, an academic "think tank" for women scholars. Her project was a study of issues confronting women at senior levels in business and the professions—those who had made it above "the glass ceiling."

And what were those issues? One word kept appearing in response to a question about the foremost challenge facing these high achievers: "Golf."

"Golf?" How could that be? But sure enough, whether the issue was bringing in business, establishing relationships with business community peers, holding on to prominent clients or socializing with fellow corporate directors, these women had figured out that the answer was "golf"—and they were determined to play.

Dawn-Marie's research and subsequent groundbreaking book on business leadership, *Members of The Club*, took her all over the country, and ultimately to Jane. Jane confirmed what Dawn-Marie had written—golf had entered the world of commerce as an international tool to heighten business and professional success. The problem was that there were still companies and executives who didn't understand how and when to use the game to their best advantage.

Well, Dawn-Marie was convinced. She decided to take

up the game but discovered that the mores of the world of golf were not entirely obvious. She was comfortable in the business world, in board rooms and in office towers, but on the golf course she needed a guide. She turned to the woman who had guided many business executives already—Jane Blalock.

INTRODUCTION

With so many new people entering the world of golf who didn't grow up in a golf environment, it is clear that some will approach the venture like a sophisticated traveler.

They are the same individuals who would not go on a business trip to Thailand or Brazil without a basic understanding of the local customs, expectations, traditions, taboos and a few key phrases. If they were planning business meetings with important clients in countries where they had not lived or visited for any length of time, they'd do a little homework. They'd ground themselves in a basic understanding of what's expected, so that when they arrived they'd be more successful. They are well aware that as travelers in a foreign land, they will be evaluated under a microscope. They will be watched and measured critically from the moment they step ashore. If they behave with grace and knowledge, they will more likely be welcomed with open arms. If they commit a faux pas, it will be noticed and remembered.

It is no different in the world of golf. Participants are judged by how they act, not by their score. In fact, golf and its advocates are perhaps more harsh than foreign business executives, who will forgive naive American visitors if they commit an error in cultural conduct. In golf you are more vulnerable—everyone watches you, every move is scrutinized, every gesture is exaggerated. The domestic business world is more forgiving—one bad day, one bad meeting, one name mispronounced does not ruin a career. There are days and meetings when an executive can even hide and act invisible. There are no such days in golf.

Business golfers who have experienced this kind of exposure—and understand the feeling of terror it can elicit—will find that the advice in this book will give them an extra advantage in their competitive world. In this book we have attempted to lay out everything a golfer needs to know about how to act—on and off the course.

As golf increasingly becomes more of a critical business tool, we think it is essential that business golfers—and indeed all golfers—give themselves the benefit of every advantage, every edge and every bit of education available. They should take advantage of the experience and wisdom of a professional who has spent her life on the golf course watching business people make mistakes—Jane Blalock.

Experienced golfers should not stop reading here. This book is not just for the novice who wants to travel confidently in a new land. There are many "ugly Americans" on the golf course who may have learned to play years ago and can boast of having low handicaps who are unaware of the mistakes they are making every day.

Thankfully, we are in an era of lifelong learning and no one understands the necessity for continuing education more than business executives who experience a dynamic and competitive environment first-hand every day. Even if they are comfortable with what they know, they make a practice of taking refresher courses to keep up with the best-practice models in their fields.

Here is our book—filled with good models for golf and business—enjoy!

ONE

THE GAME OF THE TOP FLOOR

Golf has clearly become an important tool in the business world as increasing numbers of players have taken up the sport with a passion. A recent study of golf and business executives revealed that those who play golf tend to be winners on the course and in their careers.

The executive golfers surveyed noted a definite relationship between playing the game and improving their business track record:

- ▼ 93% agreed that playing golf with a business associate is a good way to establish a closer relationship.
- ▼ 80% agreed that playing golf is a good way to make new business contacts.
- ▼ 49% agreed that the way a person plays golf is similar to how he or she conducts business affairs.

But this dry recitation of survey results does not adequately explain why so many business executives have walked onto the green. Senior executives have always played golf (or so it seems) and now the love of the game has moved to the lower floors as well—just about everyone is playing.

CEO aspirants have discovered that the golf course is a great equalizer. It brings the mail room clerk and the executive vice president to the same level—whether while teeing off or looking for a ball in the grass. The ball doesn't know or care about your title, bank account or salary, and doesn't even know your handicap.

Beyond the fact that junior executives can share the love of the game with senior executives, golf puts the player in beautiful and relaxing environments—at a leisurely pace.

Though the game inspires relaxation, business golfers must be calculating. They must be comfortable taking risks while planning every move. They must be organized, self-confident, honest, disciplined and informed—the same ingredients that create successful executives.

Golf brings out the best and worst in people, which is why many business leaders play golf with important clients, suppliers and potential hires. A round of golf offers an opportunity to build personal relationships by spending four to five hours in a relaxed setting with business colleagues who can otherwise be difficult to reach and with whom it's even more difficult to spend quality time.

As one executive said, "There really is nothing comparable to golf. In tennis, skiing, squash or sailing there is little time for conversation or a chance to get to know someone or command their undivided attention. The closest experience I can think of is riding in an airplane with a fellow executive for several hours—but even then he can read or nap."

DISCLOSURE

Perhaps the most important reason that golf is inseparable from the business world today is because it is such a good witness of one's true character. What other activity would allow you to learn the following about your golf companion?

- ▼ The speed with which she makes decisions.
- ▼ His assertiveness.
- ▼ Her response to success or failure.
- ▼ His tenacity.
- ▼ Whether she is meticulous or finicky.
- ▼ Whether he is gracious or easygoing.
- ▼ Whether she is focused.
- ▼ His level of concentration.
- ▼ How she performs under pressure.
- ▼ His integrity.
- ▼ Whether she makes excuses.
- ▼ Whether he is secure or insecure.
- ▼ Whether she is compelled to tell you how good she is.
- ▼ Whether he has a temper.
- ▼ Whether she can laugh at herself.
- ▼ How closely he follows rules.
- ▼ Whether she understands the importance of rituals.

- ▼ His intensity level.
- ▼ Her capacity for fun.
- ▼ Whether he is helpful to others.
- ▼ Whether she is bossy.

Besides providing insights into a person's character, golf is a good vehicle for face-to-face communication. In an increasingly impersonal business world, where communication typically takes place via fax, voice mail, E-mail and overnight letters, the development of personal relationships has become more valuable than ever—and those relationships can be forged on the course. Understanding the nuances of golf and the benefits it can provide in business can truly give you a competitive edge.

TIP

You can't hide from anyone else or yourself in golf. There are no impostors, no time-outs, no replays and no substitutions.

Two

People Are Talking

As executives discover golf and proceed to turn it into a whole new game, they are forthcoming with their insights as to why.

Vikki Pryor, Senior Vice President
at Blue Cross/Blue Shield:

"I basically thought golf was a boring game. But when our CEO 'suggested' I play in an upcoming tournament, I had two weeks to learn. I had never held a golf club, but I drummed up a few willing victims to take me in hand and I learned enough to keep from embarrassing myself.

"As I made it through the 18 holes of the tournament, a light bulb went on in my head—what a great opportunity to meet with busy people for long stretches of time. Too, once you play golf with someone they seem to never forget you. You could go to a seminar with someone for three days and they might not remember you, but if you play golf with them you'll probably become a personal friend.

"There's a lot of mysticism around golf. I was intimidated at first—there's so much pomp and circumstance. It was important for me to learn what the rituals are. Now I feel comfortable and I don't feel as if people are always watching me. I wish I had taken it up much earlier in my career. I've since thanked my boss for encouraging me to play. He did me a tremendous favor as a mentor and supporter. Now I play with potential customers, with people in the business community, in local tournaments and with people at work. Recently I was out playing by myself and I hit a great shot and the group in front of me invited me to move up and play with them—the first time that's happened. So I'm making real progress, even though this is my first real season of playing regularly."

VIKKI'S TIP

"Golf isn't difficult. Warm up first, loosen up, relax. The whole point is to relax, otherwise you won't hit well. Get out there and keep the ball moving. Play with fewer clubs, organize yourself before you hit, pick up the ball if you need to. Learn at a public course, which is more relaxed and forgiving than a private one. Learn the rules and the etiquette of the game and you'll do fine."

Paul O'Brien, former Chairman
of New England Telephone Co.:

"I started encouraging employees to play golf as part of a 'democratization' of New England Telephone. We were one of the first companies to use golf in sports marketing and to encourage women who felt intimidated by the game to learn to play. I felt it was important to open up the game to people who hadn't had much access to it since golf is such a big part of doing business today. We couldn't just disenfranchise part of the work force.

"Over the years we had a lot of mixers for employees and clients—concerts, dinners, shows, tennis and golf events. Nothing has been as successful as golf. There is something about the familiarity that golf allows that can't be matched. Type A people become more relaxed and others find a channel of communication that really works. It's a natural equalizer—you can have men and women, skilled and unskilled, old and young playing the same game."

PAUL'S TIP

"You don't have to do a hard sell on the golf course. The point of golf is that it provides quality time to get to know someone. The game is almost a textbook mechanism for communications and marketing. The popularization of the women's tour and the senior men's tour have opened up many more opportunities for corporations to use golf for marketing. The average corporate decision-maker is a 52 year old white male—just like the players he is watching and emulating on the course. I'd advise business people to sponsor golf events, encourage employees to take up the game and play in local tournaments, build tournaments around team competition—your clients and employees will become as enthusiastic as new converts."

Denise Desautels, Director of Brokerage Sales at Bay State Financial Services:

"In the financial services business golf is a real business tool. I didn't realize how popular it was until I tried to make appointments in the summer and was constantly told, 'He's gone for the day.' Clearly I needed access to corporate decision-makers who were all out playing golf.

"So I decided on a course of action—learn to play! Being on the wholesale side of the insurance business, my success is tied to developing personal relationships. About 98 percent of my clients are men with handicaps from 5 to 36—and each of them relishes getting out and hitting that little white ball. Golf has allowed me to be a player in an unconventional business setting. Scheduling a 30-minute meeting may be difficult, but when I offer an invitation for a round of golf there seems to be no problem securing four to five hours in a business day. Golf also gives me great access to people. At a recent program I was paired with the chairman of a Fortune 500 company.

"I prefer not to talk business on the course. Golf is a sacred time. If a client brings up business I'll respond, but I don't initiate it. I've also learned that being involved in golf is important off the course as well. If I'm in someone's office and they have golf memorabilia on the wall, I break the ice by mentioning it. Once someone knows you enjoy the game, they have something to share with you outside of your business relationship—even if they've never played with you. They might talk about a new set of clubs they just purchased or a course they just played."

DENISE'S TIP

"Don't be leery about playing with someone who is better than you. Everyone has to start somewhere. Don't wait to start playing. Take lessons from a good teaching pro so you don't compound bad habits. Be courteous, know the rules, forget about a bad hole—just pick up the ball and start again. Learn the language, it makes everyone comfort-

able. Don't be reluctant to play with people you don't know. They're playing their ball, you're playing yours. And play with better golfers when you can—it'll help you improve your game.

Mark Brennan, President
of Mark T. Brennan & Co.:

"Any little edge you can get in this competitive world is important. Often the edge is found in knowing personal details about someone or engaging in small talk with them, which you can't do in a board room. But on the golf course—when the business suits are off and your hair is down—the atmosphere is more relaxed. Golf, too, is a humbling game. Everyone is in pursuit of the same goal—to improve their own game. And everyone hits bad shots and good ones.

"Playing the game with someone is a wonderful way to bond, particularly if you are partners. During the round feelings of camaraderie build. Where else can you say, 'You really saved my butt with that shot,' or cheer someone else's great drive?

"I'm a shopping mall developer and my clients are retailers. At a recent industry conference I played golf with another developer in the same four-man team. I really got to know him and we had a great time. His company has a hospitality tent at the Ryder Cup and he invited 100 retailers to attend. There was no reason for him to invite me, but knowing how much I love the game, he did—and of course, I accepted. That never would have happened if we hadn't played together.

"So many business people play golf today that you're at a disadvantage if you don't. Going out and playing—and building relationships with the people you play with—will help you stand above competitors who are chasing the same folks for a little of their time. By golfing with them you'll have their attention for many hours—I guarantee it!"

MARK'S TIP

"You don't have to join a fancy club or even invite people to play. One of the best ways to mix business and golf is to enter one or several of the many charity golf tournaments that are held at clubs, generally on Mondays. Just enter and show up. You'll meet other business people and you'll find the camaraderie will develop and become more meaningful as you all chase the same common goal. The people you meet will remember you and will return your calls promptly."

Maria Avitabile-Stich, Vice President
and Marketing Director
at Chase Manhattan Bank:

"I never thought I would end up being famous for golf and not for my MBA! It all started for me when I was coordinating information for bank clients who were invited to golf events as our guests. There were no women on the list. Bank executives were giving me suggestions but the women weren't golfing. I knew we had important female clients that we weren't reaching.

"So when I received a package about an 'executive women's golf clinic' I asked around the bank and found there was a great deal of interest and support from women at the bank. They all knew women clients who would go. I said, 'This makes sense,' and Chase sponsored the clinic.

"The clinic was a lightning-rod moment—a huge success. Women CFOs, corporate treasurers and other female clients who had always declined invitations to golf events said yes to this one. Eighty clients were invited and 78 showed up! The energy level was terrific and everyone kept asking, 'When's the next one?'

"Now I'm known as the patron saint of women's golf at Chase because I identified a unique event for our clients that has differentiated Chase in a special way. I've never received so much press—even the president of the bank noticed. Sponsoring golf clinics has done a lot to raise our corporate profile and now I have a lot of credibility with men who golf because sponsorship has been so successful.

"As for my own game, I'm still a beginner. I go to the range and hit balls—and I won an extra game of miniature golf because I learned how to putt at the clinics!"

MARIA'S TIP

"Find the right golf event for your company and sponsor it. Make sure it is run in a first-class manner so your clients will remember it—and you—for a long time."

Peter Gallary,
Managing Director at Putnam:

"Golf is a great relationship game and most business transactions are based on relationships. The stronger the personal relationship, the better the business relationship turns out to be. At some point you're going to have a problem come up and it helps if the person you are dealing with is more than just a business associate. That's when you need to have that 'other dimension'—the one that golf allows you to develop.

"I've been playing golf for a long time—about 35 years. If you want to play golf with business peers or clients, it's important to know what you're doing. Whether in business or in golf, credibility is important. You work hard at being credible in the conference room—do the same on the golf course. Work hard at it and it will enhance your professional stature."

PETER'S TIP

"Play well enough to be credible. Take lessons. Do it the right way. Understand the language, the dress codes, the rules of conduct. There is a certain amount of etiquette required in golf. It hurts your credibility if you don't know the basics of etiquette and proper conduct."

Kevin Laura, Director of Golf Sales and Marketing at Imperial Headwear:

"I came to golf at an early age but my career opportunities blossomed in the caddie world when I became an Evans Scholar. This scholarship program for kids who were caddies is a great way for young people who are not necessarily golfers to get through school on a golf scholarship. When I got out of school I thought of being a golf pro—but I never imagined I'd find the career I now have in the world of golf. I've worked on the tournament side, running The International at Castle Pines, the Northville Long Island Classic and the Senior Players Championship in Detroit. I worked for Mazda's ad agency in sports marketing and now I'm marketing golf headwear.

"I believe golf has become so exciting and popular because it is no longer just for the elite. Everyone's playing it—the fellows in the shipping dock and the executives upstairs. Golf is becoming more affordable and the people just seem to fall in love with it.

"I'm excited that there's so much enthusiasm out there. When someone makes the effort to play they seem to get hooked. They find there's a lot more fun to the game than what they see on TV and, of course, that's good for me! As all those baby boomers age and start to lose hair, they'll need hats to cover their scalps."

KEVIN'S TIP

"Try it. Just get out there and do it. All you need is clubs, balls, a lesson and a hat! You'll love it."

THREE

SO YOU'VE DECIDED TO PLAY GOLF

If you were considering an initial public offering, would you ask your spouse for advice? If you were launching a new product, would you leave the matter of trademark protection up to your son or daughter? Learning to play golf or deciding to improve your game is an important venture, too, and unless your spouse or child is a certified golf teaching professional, don't be tempted to take lessons from them.

Although they mean well when they offer advice, you deserve professional instruction at every turn. It's hard not to take advice from those you love (not to mention your boss or client). But there's nothing wrong with politely thanking them and telling them that you'll mention their suggestion to your golf teacher at your next lesson.

TEACHER'S PET

Just as there is no particular formula for finding a personal physician, there is no single way to find a professional golf instructor. You may need to:

- Ask friends who are good golfers for their recommendations.

- ▼ Call a local private club and ask to speak with the teaching pro.
- ▼ Call the PGA or LPGA and ask for a list of certified teaching professionals in your area.
- ▼ Look in a phone book, local golf publication or national golf magazine.
- ▼ Attend a local golf school and work with a pro on staff.
- ▼ Sign up for group clinics at local clubs, courses or adult education centers.

There is legitimate disagreement about whether men should teach men and women should teach women. Some players are more comfortable with an instructor of the same sex. Others truly don't care—they are just looking for a teacher who is knowledgeable and can communicate well. Clearly many women became good golfers after taking lessons from men and, by the same token, women who are certified teaching professionals can often outplay most men on the course.

Finding the right golf instructor is a bit like dating and it's not a bad idea to follow the old rule about a blind date: "Give them more than one chance." But if the chemistry's not right after that, there's no rule that says you can't shop around for a teacher that meets your needs.

Once you have found a teacher, ask questions about his or her time availability, fees, philosophy of teaching, prior history and references from current students. Arrange several lessons and give the teacher a chance to get to know you. After a few lessons, you will be able to tell if the instructor is right for you.

Does the instructor listen to you and ask you about your lifestyle, your goals, your budget and your athletic ability? Does she adopt her teaching style to meet your needs? Does he give you homework? Does she use a video camera? Is he patient? In addition to the style of the teacher, don't forget to ask:

- ▼ What will be covered in each lesson?
- ▼ Does the teacher suggest written material?
- ▼ How long will it be before you play on a course?
- ▼ Will the teacher give lessons on the course?
- ▼ What are the teacher's philosophies and goals?
- ▼ What is the cost and the length of the lessons?
- ▼ Will she help you with club selection and fitting?
- ▼ Will you learn the rules of golf etiquette?
- ▼ Will he act as your golf advisor in the future?

WELCOME TO HARD TIMES

Don't get discouraged. There is no such thing as immediate gratification in golf. Learning the strokes takes time and if you are striving to improve to the next level it will take longer. Space your lessons out to give yourself time to practice, and consider stopping lessons for a few weeks while you take the time to play more. Keep a log of your practice sessions and rounds, noting your progress and areas that need improvement.

One rule of thumb is if you are making a change in any aspect of your game, you will have to do it 99 times to get it right once. You will inevitably encounter the temptation to revert to what you were doing before. Don't become impatient with yourself or your instructor. You must work through five levels when changing anything about your game:

▼ The ability to do it consistently in practice.

▼ The ability to do it consistently on the tee.

▼ The ability to do it consistently in a practice round.

▼ The ability to do it consistently during competition.

▼ The ability to do it under pressure.

At the end of the day, success is often up to the student. The guidelines are the same as they were in college:

✔ Be prepared for the lesson.

✔ Be on time.

✔ Stay for the whole lesson.

✔ Do your homework.

✔ Understand what the day's lesson will cover.

✔ Take notes.

✔ Ask questions.

✔ Ask for recommended supplemental help.

To find a PGA or LPGA certified instructor in your area, write the PGA at 112 T.P.C. Boulevard, Ponte Vedra Beach, FL, 32082 (904-285-3700) or the LPGA at 2570 Volusia Avenue Suite B, Daytona Beach, FL 32114 (904-254-8800).

Finally, as you begin your lessons give yourself a present and buy a golf rule book. The rules in golf are complex and precise and will take years to learn. That's why you want to own your own copy—it will last a lifetime and will make you a better golfer.

TIP

Remember what Harvey Penick said, "It is easier to learn something new than it is to unlearn something that you have been doing wrong for a long time."

FOUR

HOW GOOD DO I HAVE TO BE?

Get out there and play. Keep playing and playing and you'll improve. If you don't have time for a round, go to the driving range or practice putting on your living room rug.

We know that some players (accountants, perhaps?) will want to know a number—a precise score above which they should not venture out on the course with clients or business peers. We, however, would never advise that golfers should not participate in a round of golf because they are still beginners.

Your own comfort level in the sport may dictate the time and place at which you will make your debut. It also may depend on the format and the purpose of the event. While a friendly company outing or a charity scramble may welcome beginners, some tournaments may require proof of your minimum scores before you are allowed to participate.

No matter how well or poorly you play, the most important thing is that you understand the rules and do not slow the pace of players who are more skilled. Few golfers will mind playing with a beginners as long as they move along quickly and show respect for the game.

SEVEN

Once you've played enough golf to have a consistent record of scores on a course you will want to get a handicap. If you're not sure if you're "handicap eligible," check with your local pro or instructor.

Handicaps are important to prove a certain minimum ability if you want to play with groups of other players at certain clubs. Organizers of programs and other golf events may also ask your handicap before letting you play—so don't give yourself a handicap by not having one.

The handicap system is one reason why golf is such a good sport for business associates since it allows players of varying abilities to play together. After all, the objective of the game is to conquer the course—not your companion.

Almost all courses are rated a "par 72," which means the expectations of a scratch player (a very good one) is to shoot a 72 on 18 holes.

But there are par 72 courses and there are par 72 courses. Not all courses are created equal, so they are rated according to the degree of difficulty and given a "slope." If a player consistently shoots 85 on an easy course, he or she may have a higher handicap than a peer who shoots 85 on a very difficult course.

A low handicap correlates with a good golfer, whereas a high handicap is indicative of a less skilled golfer. A golfer's gross score on a round is his total number of actual strokes shot (for example, 105); his net score is the score after his handicap is subtracted (for example, if his handicap is 15, his net score is 90).

Simply, a handicap tells you how many strokes over par you are likely to shoot in a round of golf. Tony has a 10 handicap. Par is 72. He shoots around 82. Pam has a 20 handicap. Par is 72. She shoots around 92. The handicap can be used in "stroke play" when all strokes are counted for the round—the way most professional golf is played.

If, for instance, Pam shoots 100 (a gross score), she subtracts her handicap of 20. Her net score is 80 for the day. Tony shoots 95 and subtracts his handicap of 10. His net score is 85. If they were competing, Tony would win the gross competition with 95, and Pam would win the net competition with 80.

The handicap can also be used in "match play"—when players compete against each other on a hole-by-hole basis, winning, losing or tying each hole as the match proceeds. The winner is the player who finishes 18 holes and has won more holes than the other player. If Pam plays Tony in match play, Tony must give Pam 10 strokes. She gets one stroke for each of the 10 toughest holes on the score card. As determined by a committee, the holes are rated by degree of difficulty. The toughest hole is rated number-one handicap, to the easiest hole, number-18.

Golfers can obtain a handicap by filling out a handicap form at a golf course. With your paperwork complete, you will begin to post 18-hole scores that you shoot at a course. Carefully follow the pro's instructions about recording scores and having them signed by a companion. You must post a specified amount of scores to establish a handicap.

DANGEROUS MINDS

A word of caution: Turn in your actual scores for every round. Only registering your high numbers will give you an inflated handicap and brand you as a sandbagger. Playing with a dishonest high handicap to achieve lower net scores is like a furniture retailer advertising "50 percent off" original prices that were phony to begin with. Recording just your low scores is just as dishonest.

In some European countries you may be asked to prove your skill level by being certified on the driving range before you are allowed to play. If you are contemplating playing with business peers overseas it's a good idea to check on the requirements. On European courses, golf is considered a "privilege."

FIVE

EQUIPPING YOURSELF FOR BUSINESS

You can't buy your way to a better golf game, but having the proper equipment is an important part of your total golf package. In response to the question, "How much should I spend?" we'll counter, "How much would you spend on a business suit?"

The principle is the same. You probably wouldn't buy a business suit at a chain discount store, but you may well buy a Brooks Brothers or Armani suit at Filene's Basement instead of Saks Fifth Avenue. In either case, you dress appropriately for your position and industry so as not to embarrass yourself. You might not need top of the line labels or to spend more than you are comfortable spending, but as a new executive, you wouldn't want to create the wrong impression by wearing the wrong apparel. It's the same thing with golf equipment—you don't have to spend $2,000—but you shouldn't play with a $79 starter set.

THE PLAYER

The basic set of clubs consists of a driver, 3 and 5 woods, a putter, seven or eight different irons and two or three wedges—about 14 clubs in all. A starter set consists of a driver and one wood, a 3, 5, 7 and 9 iron, a sand wedge, pitching wedge and putter. You can certainly play with a starter set as you begin, but as you become more skilled, you may graduate quickly to needing a full set.

Having the proper equipment is critical to your enjoyment of the game. Don't:

- ▼ Buy used clubs.
- ▼ Borrow someone else's clubs.
- ▼ Buy clubs for anyone else (a gift certificate is a better idea).
- ▼ Ask to try someone else's clubs (some golfers don't like anyone even touching their clubs).
- ▼ Use one set of clubs if two people are playing.

HELP

Purchase clubs from a golf or sporting goods store or your local pro shop. If there isn't an expert there who will help fit you to clubs, go to the next store. A club-fitter should study your swing, take measurements and design the clubs to fit your swing. You will be asked to choose between a metal or wood driver (generally metal is easier to hit and lighter in weight) and between steel or graphite irons (graphite is generally more flexible and lightweight). Putters come in a blade, flange or mallet style, center-shafted or heel-shafted. Confused yet?

As you try out different clubs in the store, you'll be asked your opinion on clubhead design, clubhead lie, the type and flex of the shaft, the type and size of the grip and the weight of the club. For that reason it's a good time to ask yourself, "Am I ready to make a commitment to golf?" If you are, you might want to rent various kinds of clubs (even car rental companies now rent clubs) and practice with them first or ask to try a demo model. While the first set of clubs you buy will undoubtedly not be your last (are you still playing tennis with that wooden racquet you started with?), you'll want to make the most informed purchase you can at this stage of your play.

To do so you really have to know your own game. Do you perform better with light clubs or heavier ones? Do you have trouble getting your ball in the air? A good clubfitter will ask you many questions, watch you swing, look at your arm length and torso build, inquire about your golf goals, your frequency of play, the time investment you plan to make and your budget.

You don't have to overspend. Set a budget and choose equipment you'll enjoy. Leave the golf shop without a single guilty feeling about your decision.

SPEED BALLS

Clubs will not be your only purchase—you will want to stock up on balls. And though you might at first be motivated by price, you'll at least want to be able to talk the language of balls.

"Compression" is the "feel" sensation of the ball when it's hit. A 100 compression ball might not travel further than a ball of less compression, but it will feel different to you. Balls are also made of various materials and covered with diverse surfaces, which dictate how they roll, spin, lift and travel. The choice of balls is a matter of preference, but there are several points to remember:

Be careful about purchasing used or "water" balls.

There is no way to tell about their age or where they have been.

"X" balls or other discounted balls sell for less than the top brand label balls and may well be factory overruns or balls with slight defects. Some may have company names on them. They should be fine to use.

Take care of your balls and store them properly. Keep the ball you are using clean throughout the round.

Mark your balls with your initials or some other designation that is particular to you so there will be no confusion on the course. You must be able to identify your golf ball. Play with the same type of ball throughout the round.

Finally, a word about other equipment. Bags are like luggage—the size, weight and price are all a matter of personal preference. A "Sunday bag" is a small canvas bag that holds less than 10 clubs. Just as you would not ask to share someone else's briefcase on a business trip, it is important to have your own golf bag—and use it. It is part of your array of business tools.

TIP

If you are using the wrong equipment, your body and swing will have to overcompensate for it—which negates the effectiveness of your lessons.

SIX

MEMORIZE THIS BEFORE YOU START

You can play golf with a business peer if you are a rank beginner, but you cannot play golf with a business peer if you do not know the Ten Commandments of the game:

▼ ONE: Thou shall not talk or move or make noise while your playing partner is hitting.

This includes rattling change, candy or tees in your pocket, blowing your nose, shuffling your feet or breathing loudly. Consider the moment sacred.

▼ TWO: Thou shall not stand in back of a player.

Stand off to the side but facing your playing partner so you arc in full view. It is distracting for a player to see someone in the periphery. If you are swinging, make sure no one is close to you when you swing.

▼ THREE: Thou shall leave the course as you found it.

Rake the bunker after taking your shot, including anyone else's footprints or ball marks. Enter bunkers at the lowest point below the ball. Replace divots and repair ball marks on greens, pat down spike marks and replace the flag stick in the hole. The groundskeeper has worked hard to keep the course in top condition. Help him out.

▼ FOUR: Thou shall not stand, walk or cast a shadow in a player's putting line.

Treat the imaginary line between a ball and the cup on the green with reverence and never disturb it.

▼ FIVE: Thou shall not record your score on the putting green.

Surely you can remember your score until you walk off the green and get to your cart or bag. Yes, it's only a few seconds, but a few seconds on every hole add up.

▼ SIX: Thou shall not comment about another player's score as the round progresses.

It's like a no-hitter in baseball. You will jinx a good round by calling attention to the score.

▼ SEVEN: Thou shall be prepared.

The player with the lowest score on the previous hole has the "honor" to tee off first on the next hole. Know your scores and whether it is your turn to tee off first. The player whose ball is farthest away from the hole hits first (he is "away"); the player whose ball is closest to the flag hits or putts last and tends the flag. Know when it is your turn.

▼ EIGHT: Thou shall mark your ball before you pick it up.

If a ball is in your way on the green it may be "marked"—ask a fellow player. If you hit it, it's a two-stroke penalty. Mark the ball (by placing a coin or other marker behind the ball) before you pick it up. When you are ready to putt put the ball back and then pick up the marker.

- ▼ NINE: Thou shall not spend time looking for lost balls.

You can have a "60 second look." Although the rule allows longer, it is one you should not follow. After a minute, play a new ball.

- ▼ TEN: Thou shall not take more than one practice swing at the ball.

You can take as many practice swings as you want while someone is looking for a lost ball or while you are waiting for the group behind you to "play through." But when it is your turn to hit, do so.

TIP

If you follow the 10 commandments, you'll be a sought-after golf companion in heaven.

SEVEN

GOLF IS A MENTAL GAME

Litigators preparing for a major court battle, advertising executives designing a client presentation, financial officers readying an initial public offering or human resource managers strategizing a company-wide downsizing may think they don't have time to play golf.

They're wrong. A round of golf could be the best mental preparation possible for honing their intellectual skills for the business world.

Just as with any major business activity, the mental side of the golf game requires hard work. Business golfers should emulate the professionals they see on the course and imitate the way they prepare for a major tournament.

Think out the course and each step of each hole. Long before any of her major tournaments, Jane would spend quiet, meditative time alone. She would play the course in her mind, stroke by stroke.

BOUND FOR GLORY

Practice is an important part of mental preparation. Jane would always take a practice round on the far end of the practice tee so she would not be distracted. She practiced putting and told herself that each stroke was the "putt she needed to win," working herself into the same state of mind as if it were the final stroke of the tournament. She would attempt to feel the tournament pressure during her practice round and try to replicate the nervousness she could expect on tournament day. By doing so, she would create a sense of already having been there when she stepped up to tee off in the real event.

Making decisions about how to play the holes in advance prepares you for the real thing. Jane always held to her game plan unless major adjustments were called for, such as unexpected bad weather. Having a game plan allowed her to adapt to changing circumstances without panic or confusion. Without a compelling reason to alter her strategy, she would go ahead as planned.

Thorough preparation is as essential in golf as it is in business. Every aspect of a project, whether installing a complex computer system or driving, putting and chipping for a golf tournament, requires attention before the main event. As the important moment approaches, winning golfers use additional techniques for success.

Familiar routines help good golfers relax and maintain composure. For many years, Jane wore her "good luck clothes" and would not talk on the phone the morning of an event. If she ate a particular meal for breakfast and shot well, she'd eat the same thing the next day. Any business executive who has a favorite "meeting suit" or breakfast routine can identify with these superstitions.

NICK OF TIME

Decisiveness at key moments also is required. For example, club selection should be done with authority. It doesn't matter what club you choose but if you hit the ball with lingering indecision, you'll have a poor shot. Choose a club and stick with it. Similarly, how you play a shot or read a putt requires action. It is acceptable to change your mind, as long as you do it decisively.

Strategy, too, is essential for complete management of a golf game. Like a CEO outlining a strategic plan to her board of directors, you have to know when to be aggressive and when to play it safe. Sometimes it takes more courage to play it safe, but you must have the courage of your convictions. Just as a CEO may decide to sell a struggling but high potential product division in order to achieve more consistent profitability and maintain share price, you may hit a tee shot in the rough with an uneasy lie and a creek ahead and choose to give up a stroke to save two or three.

Mental visualization is a part of every winning golf stroke. You have to think about the shot, visualizing where you want to hit it and eliminate negative predictions about where it could land. Here are the steps: Figure out your proper yardage, select a club, stand over the ball and think one positive "swing thought." A swing takes a second and a half, so don't recreate the stroke as you perform it. Eliminate the "what ifs" and "I hopes." Instead, think: "Here's what I must do" and then do it.

PERSUASION

Good execution depends on a positive mental approach:

- ▼ Never think about winning or losing.
- ▼ Never start giving yourself the congratulatory speech as you are walking down the 18th hole.

▼ Live in the moment of the shot, the execution, the delivery.

▼ Take one shot at a time.

▼ Don't look ahead or back.

▼ Put all your energy into that one moment.

▼ Concentrate only as you address the ball—not for all 18 holes.

As in most business meetings, in a golf game there is usually a critical point in the round. It may not be the 18th hole, but a good golfer knows it instinctively. You are the only one who knows as you approach the ball which shot is the critical one for the match—just as a salesman knows the point at which a sale will close in the middle of a pitch.

A winning golfer identifies a critical moment, summons his inner resources, and responds to it. Most athletes have heard about "being in the zone." Lawyers who deliver a stirring closing argument in court experience it, entrepreneurs whose companies' stock soars experience it, retailers whose cash registers sing at Christmas experience it.

Winning golfers experience "the zone" because they are able to use their desire to succeed to overcome their fear of bad shots. They think:

✓ "I've been here before,

✓ "I can do this,"

✓ "I am going to do this!"

TIP

Winning golfers accomplish their goal because
they begin mental preparation
well before they take their first swing.
Such preparation enables them to bring intense
calmness to the game—which in turn helps them
execute their plan with a level of self-confidence
that exceeds their ability.

Eight

You've Been Invited To Play

You've taken lessons, played a few practice rounds, and your new boss has arrived on the scene. He says, "What do you say we play a round of golf next Friday."

You're not in a panic, you're ready. In fact, this is the moment you've been waiting for.

City Slickers

First things first. Take out your equipment and inspect it. Wipe off your clubs and check your golf bag. You're not leaving on a two-week vacation, so don't pack everything you own. But do make sure you have the basics:

✔ Glove (Most golfers wear them while playing, some wear them while putting, some don't. Either is all right as long as it's in a safe place when you're not wearing it—and you don't rip the Velcro apart just as your boss starts into his back swing.)

✔ Aspirin/ibuprofen.

✔ Tees—take more than enough.

✔ Divot repair tool.

- ✔ A small container of insect repellent.
- ✔ Hat/visor (show that you understand the dangers of skin cancer).
- ✔ Sunscreen—a must.
- ✔ Rain jacket or cover-up. (Leave your Burberry's at home. A lightweight, foldable rain protector will work until you get to the 19th hole.)
- ✔ Balls. (Bring plenty and put one in your pocket as well. Remember, don't spend much time searching for a lost ball—take the "60 second look.")
- ✔ Towel (a small one—not a bath or beach towel).
- ✔ Adhesive bandages (for blisters).
- ✔ Umbrella or rain cover for clubs.

With all this to carry, you see why you need your own golf bag. Sharing bags with someone else just isn't done.

READY TO WEAR

Even more than IBM in the 1950s—with its white shirts and wing tips—golf is a game of long-standing tradition in dress and protocol. While the notion of a "dress code" may seem anathema in an age of dress-down Fridays, think of the dress code as just one more part of the rich tradition of the game. Unlike the tradition of "tennis whites," however, the golf dress code hasn't changed much over the years. And unlike tennis whites, there is no official dress color, style or uniform for golf. You either know it or you don't, and your boss will either greet you with a warm handshake or an icy stare if you embarrass him by wearing the wrong thing. Worse, you will be asked to leave the premises or told to purchase appropriate attire in the pro shop. Start off on the safe side by calling the pro shop at the club where you are scheduled to play and ask:

- ▼ Are golf shoes required on the course and does the club prefer spikes or no spikes? Rules on spikes differ so check.
- ▼ Are shorts permitted? If so, what is the permissible length?
- ▼ Are collared shirts required?
- ▼ Are there any other dress code restrictions or rules you should know about?

In general, err on the side of being conservative and traditional. If you're not sure whether your closet has the proper selection, make an investment in your career and go to your local pro shop and buy an outfit—after you've received advice from a pro.

For Men:

- ▼ Slacks
- ▼ Collared shirts
- ▼ Sweaters or vests
- ▼ No denim
- ▼ No shorts (unless specifically permitted)
- ▼ No sweats, warmups or jogging outfits

FOR WOMEN:

- Slacks or knee-length shorts
- Skirts
- Collared shirts
- Sweater or vest
- No halter tops, t-shirts, tube shirts or tank tops
- No short shorts
- No tennis skirts
- No sweats, jogging suits, warmups, Lycra or exercise clothes

NINE TO FIVE

Tee time is one o'clock, your boss said, so it's best to get there at noon. If you're someone who skids into the airport parking lot 10 minutes before take-off, the timing required for a round of golf may require a little behavior modification. You have a lot to do between noon and one o'clock.

When you arrive at the club look for the "bag drop" area where you leave your clubs to be taken to the playing area. Never carry your clubs into the pro shop. At most golf courses valet service will take care of your clubs. Bring plenty of one and five dollar bills to tip the person who takes your clubs. The more generous you are, the more the staff will treat you with reverence and the more impressed your boss or future golf companions will be. Next, go park your car.

Return to the club and ask directions to the ladies or mens locker room. This is where you will change into your golf shoes—it's tacky to change in the parking lot. If you are a guest at a private club the locker room attendant may provide you with a locker. If not, it's acceptable to change your shoes in the locker room and leave your street shoes under the bench while you play. After tipping the locker room attendant several dollars, ask if there are any club restrictions about wearing golf shoes in certain areas. The rules vary at each club.

Warming up before the round is a tradition of the game—and a good one. The warm-up includes stretching, hitting a few irons, woods, chips and putts at the driving range and putting green.

Don't forget to walk around the club before you play. Familiarity with the layout, pro shop, grille and history of the place will make your round of golf more enjoyable.

THE LONGEST DAY

Your boss is pleased that you're on time and introduces you to a few of the members. This is his club and everything from the balls on the driving range to the drinks after the round will be charged to his account. Don't mention reimbursement. You can reciprocate later—even if you don't belong to a club—by buying him the new golf book that was just published or by doing a favor for his wife. Still, a gracious acknowledgment of enjoyment at the end of the day is sufficient.

From this point on, you are in your boss' hands. Take your lead from him regarding issues of wagering, gimmie's and ready golf. Don't talk business unless he raises the subject—and enjoy the game!

There are three key phrases you need to keep in mind: CONSIDERATION, COMMON SENSE, THOUGHTFULNESS.

While transgressions of etiquette in golf are as serious as those at a formal dinner party, especially if you are playing with purists, you are less likely to make a mistake if you err on the side of politeness.

TIP

It's not how you play that is important, but how you handle yourself.

"MIND IF WE PLIÉ THROUGH?"

NINE

YOU'VE INVITED SOMEONE TO PLAY

You haven't called them yet, but you're thinking about it. A client, a prospective client, a fellow board member of your trade association, a potential new hire, a major donor to your favorite charity—each one deserves your undivided time and attention. What better way to achieve that than a game of golf?

You don't know if she plays, but you suspect she does. It is perfectly appropriate to inquire. "I was thinking of setting up an informal round of golf next month, and I can't recall if you play. Would you like to go out sometime?"

If the response is a self-deprecating, "I do play, but not very well," your proper response should be a sentence that puts the person at ease. "That's the beauty of golf—you don't have to play well to enjoy it. Let's give it a try. There is nothing that says you can't pick up the ball and go on to the next hole if you're approaching double figures."

RISKY BUSINESS

Before you open calendars and check for an agreeable date and time, call your club and make sure that you can arrange a round. We have known too many embarrassed golfers who arranged an all-important golf date only to discover the club was closed for a special tournament or event. Worse yet, we know of several incidents where golfers invited female clients to play at a club that had restricted tee-times, memberships or outright prohibitions on female guests. Jane was once invited to meet a fellow golfer at a club in Europe and when she arrived, she was rudely hustled out of the parking lot. Pl-l-l-e-a-s–e don't tell us you didn't know. Check it out.

Make your inquiries and then arrange the date and tee time. By now you know how to arrange tee times either at your municipal course or your open-to-the-public private course. If you do not have a foursome, stipulate when you call that there will only be two of you, and request that no one else be allowed to play in your group (generally allowed at private clubs but not always at a public course). Let the pro know that you will be paying for all greens fees and carts and that you will be bringing a guest. Ask if there is anything your guest needs to know.

Have you checked off everything you want to tell your guest?

✔ Directions to the club.

✔ Club phone number.

✔ Dress code.

✔ Availability of rental clubs.

✔ Where to park.

✔ Where and when to meet.

✔ Whether you will be practicing before the round.

✔ The names of the other players in your group.

Finally, be clear about how long you would like to stay (or are able to stay). If you want to have drinks or dinner with your guest after the round, make sure your guest understands and has agreed. There is nothing worse than having avoided any discussion of business for 18 holes—saving such conversation for dinner—and then have your guest say, "Thanks, I've got to be going now, I've got a 6 p.m. board meeting downtown." Clear communication prevents misunderstandings.

Reconfirm the reservations at the club the day before and reconfirm with your guest.

Arrive at the club a half hour before your guest. Tip the locker room attendant a couple of dollars, give her your guest's name and ask that she be taken care of.

SPEED

Find out whether your club allows walking the course or using pull carts. Does it require motorized carts or are there caddies available?

If your club has caddies, use one. Usually a club will classify its caddies and the price varies for each. Ask the caddie master what the fee is and what an appropriate tip will be. If you have a choice of using a caddie, hire one—by all means. He or she can be a good guide to the course, pointing out terrain, yardages and other aspects of the course that will improve your game—as well as the whole experience.

If you are using carts, make sure you are comfortable driving one. If not, take it for a short practice drive before your guest arrives. Start slowly, make sure your guest is firmly seated before you proceed and be sure to set the parking brake firmly when you stop

Find out the rules of your club regarding the use of carts. You might be required to stay on cart paths only. If this is the case, you must stay on the path unless you are letting another cart pass you.

To save time on the course pull your cart up halfway between the balls on the fairway so that after you have played the ball you can walk forward to the cart.

Some clubs have a 90-degree rule, which means that carts are allowed on the fairway near the ball but they cannot be driven at any angle to the ball. They must be driven in a straight line from the cart path to the ball at a 90-degree (or right) angle from the path.

Unrestricted, or no rules, does not really mean no rules. It is never appropriate to drive carts on the green or on the fringe, near bunkers or water hazards.

As far as what else you should know about carts, rely on common sense and courtesy. And always remember:

- ▼ Take several clubs with you from the cart if you are not sure which one you will use to hit your ball—such a habit will save time.
- ▼ Do not park the cart in a player's sight line as he swings—it's distracting.
- ▼ Do not make unnecessary noise when someone else is ready to swing—releasing the brake, putting your clubs back into your bag, talking loudly. At last, you're ready to play!

TIP

Be as gracious to your guest on the course as you would be in your home.

TEN

YOU'RE ON THE COURSE

You've arrived at the golf course, changed into your shoes and are ready to go. Check with the starter before heading to the first tee. Be ready long before your exact tee time and recognize that tee time means that one member of your party will swing at that precise time, not the time that you will come skidding into the parking lot.

Be ready. Have extra balls in your pocket and take more than one club with you. Put your scorecard and pencil in your pocket and step up to the tee. Make a note of what kind of ball you are playing with so that there is no confusion later. Announce the brand name and number.

At the first tee you can use any system you'd like to determine who swings first—from a coin toss to "age before beauty." After the first shot, whoever has the ball that is farthest away from the hole shoots first. The person with the lowest score on the first hole has the honor of going first on the next one. If the score is tied, one of the players with the lowest score keeps shooting first until someone "takes the honor away" by posting a lower score.

During crowded course conditions, or if your group is lagging behind, it may be a good idea to play "ready golf"—whoever reaches the tee first and is prepared to swing does so. Don't imitate genteel businessmen in a high rise office elevator who gesture "after you" to ladies stuck in the back of the crowd. Step off with alacrity.

Before you swing, look ahead. Wait until the group that has teed off in front of you is far enough away that there is no possibility of hitting them or interrupting their play. If some—but not all—are clearly out of range, you should let your shorter hitters tee off first.

We are strict on practice swings at the tee. We could probably forgive one—but only one. The time to practice is at the driving range before the round. Imitate professional basketball players. They do not step out onto the court when the buzzer sounds and take their first shot of the day from mid-court or the free-throw line. They have practiced those shots during the warm-up session because they know they will not do their best in the real game if they are "cold." If you do take additional practice swings during the round, be courteous enough to refrain from doing so while others are taking their real swings. That is the time to stand still and be quiet.

After the first player has hit, the next one should step up quickly and hit, and so on. The idea isn't to play fast, but efficiently. Try not to waste time or motion. Take extra clubs with you when it's your turn to hit instead of walking back to the cart for another. By the same token, position the cart ahead of your ball or the green so you don't have to retrace your steps to move forward.

We do not recommend "Mulligans"—those "free" second swings. Golf is not tennis where you are allowed two serves. If you are in a friendly game and your business peers insist on allowing you a Mulligan, take it on the first tee only. Mulligans are against all golf rules. As is the case with many rules, however, there are exceptions, such as if you purchase the right to take a Mulligan during a charity tournament. Too, if the ball falls off the tee before you hit it, you can replace it. But if you swing and miss the ball entirely it counts as a stroke.

It's important to remember not to hit into the group ahead of you. Even if you do not hit them with an errant ball, it is jarring to find a stranger's ball plop among those of your group. A word about manners:

▼ Don't comment on another player's strokes or ask what club he used.

▼ Don't blame a flubbed shot on circumstances.

▼ Don't throw your club, swear or act boorishly.

▼ Don't relive a bad shot.

A MONTH BY THE LAKE

As you proceed down the fairway there are certain essentials you must remember about leaving the course in better condition than which you found it. Treat the golf course the same way you would a friend's condominium at a vacation resort that you've been invited to use for the weekend—you wouldn't dare leaving it in anything but pristine shape!

▼ Do not to allow your club to touch the ground in a water hazard or a sand trap until you swing.

▼ Enter and leave sand traps from the low side.

▼ Rake all sand traps or bunkers.

▼ Put the rake back where you found it.

- ▼ Replace divots (those pieces of turf that were torn up by your club during a swing) by patting the ground with a divot repair tool. On some courses, however, course managers would prefer that you fill in the holes with sand. Make sure you know which is the case.

- ▼ If your ball has gone out of bounds (generally marked off with white stakes or other indications) or if your ball lands in someone's back yard, you must play another ball from the place where you hit the first one. You must record a penalty for the hole you have incurred the out-of-bounds swing, and one for the second ball (stroke and distance).

At last, you are reaching the green, that wonderfully smooth and serene circle of perfectly cut grass where the hole and its flag reside.

WHERE ANGELS FEAR TO TREAD

Nothing should be on the green except you, your ball and a putter. The cardinal rule of moving on a green is "don't walk in another person's line." This means not to step on the turf that lies between another person's ball and its line to the hole. Too, be careful not to let your shadow fall in someone else's line when they are attempting their shot.

The first person to reach the green or the person whose ball is farthest from the hole should putt first. The person whose ball is closest to the pin tends the flag by holding it at arm's length from the hole. You can also leave the flag in if you want to use it as a visual target as long as a playing partner or caddie is tending the pin—but it must be removed as the ball is approaching the hole. If you are tending the flag, don't stand too close to the hole or you'll make spike marks that could affect the path of the ball. (Hint: tug on the flag stick first to make sure it will come out easily when the ball rolls near the cup.)

If there is a ball in the way of your line to the hole, it should be marked. If you hit it, it's a two-stroke penalty. Mark the ball first by placing a coin behind it before you pick it up. The ball also can be cleaned at this point. When you put the ball back, make sure you leave the coin in place until the ball is positioned correctly on the green.

Continuous putting is permissible in order to save time —as long as you are not standing in someone else's line. A player whose ball is farthest from the hole swings first and keeps playing his ball until it's in the cup. When your ball reaches the cup, you should pick it up quickly and move away.

Players can also give each other "gimmies"—a stroke that is counted but not actually swung. If your ball is so close to the cup that you couldn't possibly miss the shot, your companion may say, "that's a gimme" (but again, only in a friendly game!).

Fix any slight indentations in the grass your ball may have made when it hit the green with a ball repair tool or tee (never use your hands). Also be sure to replace the flag stick. The groundskeeper has worked hard to keep the green in perfect condition—attentive golfers try to leave it in better condition than they found it.

Once all players have finished, move quickly off the green so the group behind you can play the hole. Once you are a sufficient distance from them, record your scores while they are fresh in your mind.

DUMB AND DUMBER

There are still some golfers who may not know that the courteous thing to do is to allow a group behind them to "play through" or move ahead of them—particularly if it is a small group or the hole ahead is free. While you may be tempted to not give up your position on the course, be alert to the group coming along behind you and give way if the circumstances warrant it. It is easier to let another group play through than to get a rubber neck by constantly worrying about the folks behind you.

If, on the other hand, you are playing in a group that is marching ahead on an apparently slower foursome ahead, you may have to be patient and take in the scenery since you do not have an automatic right to play through. It might just be the case that the group ahead is held up by the players ahead of them. You should also not jump to conclusions about their speed of play by watching their balls. We have seen beginning golfers play quite quickly, as well as many occasions where the most experienced golfers are the slowest on the course.

If the opportunity to cede position does arise, however, the most appropriate places to do so are at the turn (where the front nine meets the back nine) and on the green.

NETWORK

By now you realize that golf creates friendships, shared experiences and camaraderie. It does not, however, result in business deals, promotions or strategic alliances.

If you are playing golf with a business peer, do not mention business. This bit of advice may seem out of sync in a book that touts golf as an effective professional tool. But the plain fact of the matter is that many serious golfers take great offense if a word of business intrudes on their enjoyment of the game. Take your cue from your fellow golfer. If she raises the subject of a business matter you can pursue it. But generally discussion of business should wait until the "19th hole," the time and place golfers relax and enjoy a bit of refreshment after the round.

Even at the 19th hole, however, protocol reigns. An appropriate initiative may be, "I've enjoyed this round with you and I'd like to talk sometime about how we might do business together. Can I call you next week to set up a convenient time to get together?" Some clubs have clear rules forbidding business talk on the premises, just as some eating establishments have rules prohibiting papers or documents of any kind on a table during mealtime. When in doubt, choose the conservative course of conduct.

ELEVEN

BETTING ON THE GAMES

It won't be long before you have graduated from playing simple rounds of golf to entering local charity tournaments or participating in company outings. In those cases you might find yourself playing a game within a game—and wagering on the outcome—just to make the experience more exciting.

To protect your wallet and your self-esteem, know the lingo and the rules before you eagerly agree to the terms of the competition.

THE HUSTLER

Medal Play is the most common. Here you add up the total number of strokes taken and the lowest score wins.

Match Play is a hole-by-hole competition against a certain competitor. The one who scores the lowest on each hole wins that hole.

Scramble is a format in which all the players tee off together. The second and subsequent strokes are then taken by all the players from the location of the ball in the best position to the hole. This form of play may sound like a "best ball," and if someone insists it is, bet him money on it. You'll win.

Best ball is a format in which each player plays his own ball throughout the round but the best score of the foursome on each hole is recorded as the team score for that hole.

Skins is similar to match play in that it is a hole-by-hole competition. But in the case of a tie, the contest carries over to the next hole in which there is not a tie score.

OTHER PEOPLE'S MONEY

Betting on golf has long been part of the friendly golf culture and is a common element of the game. Betting is not without its risks, however. While it adds excitement to the game (particularly if you are a competitive person), the additional pressure of lost money hovering over each stroke adds tension.

In some cases a high scorer is intensely aware that his performance may cost his team some money; whereas in another scenario, a golfer may lose concentration on his stroke while he wrestles with the ethical question of whether to win or lose to a valued client or prospective employer.

Whatever the case or dilemma may be, there is one cardinal rule about wagering in golf—PAY OFF YOUR BETS IMMEDIATELY.

If you forgot to bring your wallet to the course, don't bet. It's considered bad form to engage in betting and then not pay.

KNOW YOUR BETS:

A nassau is comprised of three bets: a bet for the first nine holes, a bet for the second nine holes and a bet for the entire 18 holes. A two-dollar nassau bet could cost you a total of six dollars.

A skins bet is a way of accumulating a pot. If the bet is a dollar skin on every hole, whoever wins the first hole wins a dollar, and so on. However, if there is a tie score on a hole, the dollar rolls over to the next hole—allowing the winner of that hole to pocket two dollars.

A press requires a full wallet. If your companion says, "Let's have an automatic press when two down," it means a new bet starts after the press is issued and the first bet continues. The person who is down has the option to press. For example, if you are betting two dollars a hole and you have lost the first two holes and the third hole is an automatic press, you then start a second betting round on that hole. If you win holes three and four, you are even money for the first bet and ahead four dollars for the press.

CASINO

There are no absolute guidelines about how much money to wager on a game of golf but a rule of thumb is not to bet less than two dollars or else you'll come across as a tightwad. Five dollars (or a drink at the 19th hole) is a perfectly acceptable maximum. If you're feeling pinched by the cost of lessons, clubs and greens fees, there's no reason to be pressured into bets you can't cover without sacrificing your mortgage payment—no matter who is in your foursome. The golf course is not a place to show off with braggadocio—save it for Las Vegas.

TIP

Be a gracious winner and an even more gracious loser.

TWELVE

NOW YOU'RE A SPONSOR

Conventional wisdom once had it that if the CEO of a company was a golfer, the company sponsored golf tournaments. If she was a tennis enthusiast, the company sponsored tennis tournaments. The marketing staff learned to read the sporting interests of the occupant of the corner office and spend accordingly.

Not any longer. Today's marketing professionals are savvy about what events to sponsor and about how to evaluate the benefit to the company—especially since costs have increased many fold and the return on a company's investment can be quantified.

Whether you're a CEO, a product manager, mass marketer, public relations executive, special events coordinator, advertising manager or marketing chief, it's more than likely that you'll be presented with an opportunity to sponsor a golf event.

Today all organizations are looking for nontraditional ways to attract the attention of key decision-makers. If part of your business strategy is to reach a particular income, demographic or psychographic group, sponsoring a golf tournament may be a very effective marketing fit.

If your company has a fixed amount of money to spend,

how will you decide whether investing in a golf sponsorship will be cost effective? First you have to decide who your target audiences are—marketing 101.

Perhaps you are a new director of the Chamber of Commerce, and co-sponsorship of the Chamber's annual tournament will establish your presence as a leader in the business community.

Perhaps you are about to be named the next chairman of the board of a local charity and it would be beneficial for your company to obtain local visibility by sponsoring the charity's first golf fund-raiser.

Perhaps you are head of business services for a regional telecommunications company and you need to reach a key group of senior level corporate decision-makers as you launch a new product.

Perhaps a national golf tournament is being held in your city for the first time—a once-in-a-decade opportunity for your company to receive national visibility and to host your most important clients at a prestigious event.

Whether the event is a sanctioned tournament associated with one of golf's national professional organizations, a one-day program tournament or a local charity fundraiser, there will be several levels of sponsorship with varying pricing structures—depending on the audience and reach of the tournament:

- Title sponsor
- Host sponsor
- Presenting sponsor
- Associate sponsor
- Media sponsor

- Official sponsor
- Corporate patron

All of these sponsorship levels could be offered to local and national companies.

Many of the sponsorship packages will include hospitality tents, program advertisements, tickets and other marketing enhancements.

Key questions to ask include:

- Will the company name be visible?
- Do you want the company name to be visible?
- Where and for how long?
- Does the cost include on-site visuals or does the company have to provide them?
- What else does the cost of sponsorship include?
- Is the company managing the event a professional golf marketing firm and does it have a reputation for excellence?
- Is it important for the company to have control over how the event is run?
- If a charity is involved, what percentage of the revenues will it receive?
- How much recognition will the company receive?
- What will be required of the company and its staff?

THE CLIENT

Marketing professionals, product managers and others who have tuned into the economic drawing power of golf will eventually consider the benefits of initiating their own golf tournament—whether a public event for a charity or organization tied to the company or a private function for the company's sales representatives or most valued customers. While the allure of standing in front of a microphone welcoming a coterie of the community's most distinguished business and civic leaders to your company's event may sound appealing, a word of caution is required. The following are some of the horror shows we have seen:

- Payments are made to a celebrity golf professional who doesn't appear.
- Gift bags do not arrive at the right location.
- The club enforces discriminatory policies against women and minorities.
- The club has scheduled another event for the same day.
- Name tags are misspelled.
- The photographer forgets his film.
- The golf carts are locked up as participants arrive—with no key in sight.
- The golf carts have no gas.
- Volunteers do not show up to assist.
- There is no one to carry bags from the drop off area to the starting tee.

- ▼ The facility has no rental clubs for guests.
- ▼ There is no company banner at the front gate—or anywhere else.
- ▼ Volunteers are still setting up as guests arrive to register
- ▼ An important message for a distinguished guest is not delivered
- ▼ The Waterford trophy is lost.
- ▼ There is no contingency plan for bad weather.
- ▼ Loud construction noise is heard as the guest speaker begins to talk.

The best way to avoid horror shows as these at your tournament is to hire a golf event marketing company with a sparkling track record. Seek recommendations from business executives who have experienced great results from the firms they've used. Months of preparation and attention to detail often are required to ensure that a golf event conforms to the highest standards possible. Once the planning for the event is in capable hands, a chairman of a tournament should have no problems sleeping—knowing that every contingency is being considered.

AN AFFAIR TO REMEMBER

It is entirely appropriate to interview representatives of several event management companies and ask them for detailed proposals and references. Do not base your final decision on price, however, without understanding the nuances of the work involved and the expertise of the staff who will be carrying it out.

When you begin searching out candidates, consider the following about the companies you're looking at:

- ✔ How many golf events has it managed?
- ✔ Does it have experience running your type of event? (A golf outing is different than a golf clinic or tournament. A fund-raising tournament is different than a client tournament or company outing.)
- ✔ Does its staff include golfers who understand what is involved in producing such an event?
- ✔ Does it have access to (or a professional relationship with) golf touring pros or teaching pros to put on clinics or demonstrations at the event?
- ✔ Does it have access to suitable golf courses, clubs or facilities for your event?
- ✔ Will it arrange the exclusive use of the course, club or facility on the days you request?
- ✔ Can it handle an out-of-town event—including travel, accommodations, transportation, shipping materials and local on-site liaisons?
- ✔ How many people will it have on site and will they be experienced employees or volunteers?
- ✔ Will its executives work with your company on marketing the event? Public relations? Packages for sponsorship?
- ✔ Will it work with your company to advertise and promote the event?
- ✔ Will it handle the media? Does it have media contacts?

- ✔ Will it develop and protect the event's trademark or logo?
- ✔ Will it produce and sell event merchandise?
- ✔ Will it screen and hire a keynote speaker?
- ✔ Will it arrange appearances by celebrity golf professionals or other special guests?
- ✔ Will it produce and provide the on-site visuals and other signage?
- ✔ Will it handle the R.S.V.Ps?
- ✔ Will it handle the pairings (including golf cart assignments), scoring and rules?
- ✔ Will it coordinate registrations—including last-minute pairing changes?
- ✔ Will it secure prizes and coordinate gift bags?
- ✔ Does it have ideas about highly desirable products for the gift bags?
- ✔ Will it handle insurance and liability issues?
- ✔ Will it provide contingency plans for unpredictable circumstances such as bad weather?
- ✔ Will it work with the club or facility management and staff to make sure the on-site details of your event are handled efficiently—including traffic and parking?
- ✔ Will it execute contracts?
- ✔ Will it handle money matters such as deposits and bills?

TIP

A first-class event management company can handle every aspect of your golf event, help you maximize public exposure and present the corporate image you desire to your targeted audience.

THIRTEEN

HOSPITALITY TENTS

At a golf tournament or event, companies often entertain guests in hospitality tents purchased from the event's producers or organizers. Less expensive than full-scale sponsorship, hospitality tent packages may include a certain number of tickets and parking passes to the event. If you don't care about having your company's name up in lights for national television cameras, a hospitality tent is an effective way for executives to entertain important clients, potential clients, suppliers and other key business peers.

Purchasing a hospitality tent at a golf event involves analyzing the price, the product and the return on your investment—as is the case with any marketing decision. Ask additional questions as well:

✔ Will the company be able to buy tickets or ground passes in addition to those included in the package?

✔ Will food and liquor be included in the price of the tent? If not, is there a food and liquor supplier that must be used?

✔ Will there be a security staff checking credentials?

✔ Will the company need to supply its own badges or credentials for guests?

The thought processes for organizing a company hospitality tent is similar to those which go into orchestrating any other company event. If the sales organization has been given tickets to give to favored customers, anticipated revenues and other measures of return can be assigned as quotas. Companies have used hospitality tents for announcements of a new product line or service, an executive appointment or a new acquisition.

When they are used for company-sponsored golf events, often celebrity guests are invited and photographs are taken of attendees with the celebrity. If a hospitality tent is well organized, every guest will enjoy the event—not just golf enthusiasts.

All guests invited to the event should be selected—and treated—with great care. Invitations should include directions, agenda, dress code, a description of the event and the names of top company executives.

Company executives should be well prepared as hosts. They should be briefed with the names and biographies of the guests who will be attending each day. Senior executives should be available at all times and as accessible and personable as they would be in their own homes. Guests should be given gift bags (in which company promotional material may be included).

Remember, the clients and customers you are inviting to your hospitality tent have no doubt been invited to other tents. They compare details—from the food and gift bags to the presence and graciousness of company executives—so put your best foot forward. If you don't have any experience using hospitality tents for corporate entertainment, consider hiring an event management firm to help you maximize the value of your purchase and oversee important details.

GUESS WHO'S COMING TO DINNER

As a guest you have less responsibility than the executives who organized the function, but the standards of business conduct you must uphold are just as high. You have been invited for a reason and should act like the VIP the company host considers you to be.

✔ Dress correctly. Polo shirts, blazers, chinos, dresses or coordinated pant outfits are best. No blue jeans, shorts or T-shirts.

✔ Meet the person who invited you.

✔ Arrive when expected.

✔ If you can't make it, give notice in advance.

✔ Be polite to your hosts.

✔ Know the names of company executives and speak to them.

✔ Show interest in the company.

✔ Converse about the event and its importance.

✔ Graciously accept what is offered.

✔ Don't use the occasion to fill up on freebies.

✔ Send a thank you note to the person who invited you. Gestures of appreciation are noticed and go a long way to establish effective and lasting business relationships.

SUDDENLY LAST SUMMER

A major golf tournament has come to your area and you find yourself the lucky recipient of an invitation. Watching golf tournaments is a great pleasure and, as with all great events, has its own standard of conduct.

Golf is more like tennis than football. Spectators must be absolutely quiet—good shots are rewarded with polite applause, if anything. The thrill of observing a golf tournament and some of the game's most famous players is to learn by witnessing them in action—including observing their quiet concentration.

As a spectator you will be within close range of the players, but it is not appropriate to speak to them until the round is over and they have signed their scorecards. It may look as though they are not concentrating when they are walking from hole to hole or waiting for a fellow player to swing—but they are. Just as you would not approach a tennis pro during a changeover between games of a tight match, do not approach a golfer until the event has ended.

There are two ways of enjoying a golf tournament. The first is to follow a player from hole to hole, walking along the edges. The second is to pick a spot on the fairway and watch players come by and play the hole. Experienced tournament-goers also watch their favorites warm up at the driving range. In any case do not move a muscle while any player is preparing to hit. Whether you are walking or standing, stay absolutely motionless.

Tournaments are held in all kinds of weather—so be prepared. Bring a windbreaker and rain hat as well as a visor and binoculars. Check the rules about cameras—they may not be allowed during the actual event.

TIP

Hospitality tents and golf tournaments provide a cost-effective vehicle to entertain a number of important clients in a first-class way.

FOURTEEN

YOU'RE INVITED TO A PRO-AM

Every professional golf tournament starts with a pre-tournament called a pro-am—a round of competition wherein a professional is teamed with a group of amateurs. To an amateur, the chance to play in a pro-am is often the golf experience of a lifetime. Then, of course, there is the extensive marketing and promotional value of the event.

Passionate golfers eagerly pursue pro-am opportunities. In some cases golfers are invited to play by the corporate sponsor of the tournament. In other cases pro-am spots are sold by the sponsor or promoter of a charity beneficiary to raise money. Pro-am spots also can be sold as a part of a promotional package that is combined with corporate hospitality opportunities, signage, advertising or with television time. The packaging and sale of pro-am spots vary with each event, as does the price to attend.

A typical national tournament sponsor, for example, may reserve most of the pro-am slots for its top customers and give the rest to a charity. It is not uncommon for an amateur to pay up to $10,000 to play with a pro.

The format of the pro-am also varies according to each tournament's rules. There may be a maximum handicap allowed for participants. The game could be a scramble or follow a best ball format with tee times running all day. It could even follow a shotgun format.

Groupings of amateurs and pros might be arranged by request (if you've paid for three spots and want to play with your two most valued clients). Groupings also could be based on ability—creating groups of approximately equal skill and handicap. As in the tournament itself, prizes are given and play is competitive.

Pro-ams have become so popular with golf enthusiasts that they've taken on a life of their own. Often celebrities, diplomats and government leaders are invited to increase the drawing power of a pro-am—adding to the excitement and glamour. In some cases celebrity attendance has drawn a bigger spectator crowd at the pro-am than the tournament itself!

BEAUTY AND THE BEAST

Playing in a pro-am can test the nerves of the calmest golfer—but that need not be the case. A professional golfer does not expect his amateur companions to play as well as he does. He or she is well aware that they may be nervous—especially on the first tee. Pros are accustomed to playing in pro-ams—it's part of their job. It is also part of their job to make amateurs feel comfortable, although some are better at it than others.

If you have the chance to participate in a pro-am try to get the most out of it. Read the invitation carefully and make sure you understand the format. Show up early to ensure yourself the opportunity to mingle with the other players. Take time to warm up. If there is a clinic prior to the event you are best advised to participate.

Get to know your pro as you play but remember that the main objective is to play golf and enjoy the camaraderie. The other amateurs in your group may be as nervous as you are. As one CEO once said, "I can address a group of a thousand employees for three hours with no problem—but I am totally miserable during the first tee of a pro-am." However, that same CEO has since come to love pro-ams—finding that most pros are ordinary people and are willing to share a tip or two about the game.

Jane has played in many pro-ams and observes that amateurs hold the key to whether the day is a glorious one or a dud. In the worst case scenarios, amateurs drag down the whole event with their nervousness, or the event is dominated by one participant who insists on acting as team captain— helping everyone with their strokes and organizing the group like a troop leader. As a pro, she finds herself in the awkward position of wanting to tell them to "shut up" but having to act gracious because they have so paid dearly to play in the event.

In the best scenarios—and the majority of them are good—the day is one of cementing personal relationships and beginning new friendships with golfers who enjoy all aspects of the sport, including its tradition for courtesy. Jane has met some of her dearest friends and most valuable clients while playing in pro-ams.

A STAR IS BORN

If the prospect of playing in a national pro-am seems out of reach, look closer to home. There are literally thousands of local pro-ams—organized by charities, corporations or associations—held at golf clubs in every community (often on Mondays, when clubs are closed or slow). These events attract all levels of pro golfers—from retired stars to local teaching pros. Creating your own pro-am has become a commonplace activity for business executives, sales organizations, marketing professionals and charity fund-raisers and, thanks to the expertise of sports management organizations, requires little effort on the part of the sponsors.

Every year Jane sponsors her own pro-am for the University of New Hampshire in which friends and alumni of the university pay to play with a group of pros.

She has several tips for those thinking of creating a pro-am event:

▼ Decide how much you want to spend to sponsor the event. Golf pros are paid to attend and play in pro-am events. They are available at all levels and prices.

▼ Decide how much participants will be willing to pay to play in such an event or whether they will be invited to play as guests (as in the case of a corporation sponsoring a pro-am event for its sales representatives or most valued clients—or any other particular marketing objective).

▼ Use the services of a sports management firm to help organize the event—according to your budget and promotional goals. It can more easily hire golf pros, arrange their contracts, transportation, accommodations and payment, as well as handle the other thousands other details required to put on a first-class event.

FIFTEEN

TALK THE TALK

Success at using golf effectively as a business tool will be determined in part by your ability to present yourself as an individual who is serious and respectful of the nuances of the game—including its terminology. Just as you would not run your nails across a blackboard at a company meeting, in golf you should not:

- ✔ Use golf as a verb. You will be giving yourself away as a novice if you say, "Do you golf?" Golf is a game that you play.
- ✔ Use golfing as a noun. You are not going golfing—you are going to play golf.
- ✔ Speak on the golf course when someone is playing. The golf course is an escape from business and the world that is too much with us. Think of it as a sacred place, a retreat.

CLUELESS

Learning the jargon and talking television golf around the water cooler can take you a long way. Know the names of some of the game's most famous:

Players: Jack Nicklaus, Patty Berg, Ben Hogan, Patty Sheehan, Arnold Palmer, Nancy Lopez, Fred Couples, Pat Bradley.

Courses: Pebble Beach, Augusta National, St. Andrews in Scotland.

Architects: Donald Ross, Tom Fazio, Jack Nicklaus, Robert Trent Jones, Rees Jones.

Resorts or areas: Pinehurst, Hilton Head, Palm Springs, the Broadmoor.

- ✔ Watch television and understand the importance of such events as the U.S. Open, the British Open, the Masters and the PGA and LPGA Championships.
- ✔ Listen to the commentators and color analysts as they describe the players and the challenges of the course. These experts know what they are talking about and can give you a good living-room seminar on the subtleties of the game.
- ✔ Watch the details of course etiquette in motion as players step carefully around the green, rake the bunkers and stand quietly while their fellow players putt.
- ✔ Attend golf tournaments. Stand at the driving range and watch how the pros swing. Then pick a spot on the course and watch the players play through. Or better yet, volunteer at a golf tournament and participate in the excitement yourself.

✔ Read, read, read. *Golf*, *Golf Digest* and *Golf For Women* magazines, Harvey Penick's classic books and the sports pages of your daily newspaper will keep you up-to-date on theory, instructional tips and the names of contemporary players.

TIP

Knowing who won the playoff last Sunday can be a conversational icebreaker!

SIXTEEN

CUTTING THE GRASS CEILING

As women continue to gain prominence as a powerful, recognizable force in the public and private sectors, they are discovering that golf gives them another arena in which to excel. Women CEOs, general counsels, mayors and senior vice presidents of sales are playing golf routinely with clients and business peers.

But it is not just senior level women who are picking up clubs. Young women starting out in business are discovering that knowing how to play the game gives them a distinct advantage over their corporate peers.

Women entrepreneurs are finding that important personal business relationships can be forged on the golf course. Women-owned businesses now employ more people than the Fortune 500 companies, and they are the fastest growing segment of new business startups. These businessowners are serious about success and about the game.

Women are not daunted by the history of golf as a male-dominated sport. In fact, women are now America's newest golf enthusiasts. According to the National Golf Foundation, roughly one-fourth of all new players since 1990 have been women. By the year 2000, half of all new players will be women. Today many of these women are in professional, managerial and administrative positions and they have lifted the ranks of women golfers to well over the six million mark.

WORKING GIRL

More often than not women are taking up golf for business reasons. As women climb the corporate ladder—or jump off the ladder and start their own business—they need to entertain clients. They need to develop relationships with suppliers. They need to meet business peers. Like their male counterparts, female business professionals are realizing a round of golf is a great way to network and build relationships. Golf is particularly advantageous for women, because:

- ▼ Players of any skill level can play together.
- ▼ It is a safe sport and takes place in safe locations.
- ▼ It is a good subject for conversation.
- ▼ There are rules and protocols that govern the conduct of the players.
- ▼ The social skill in golf is just as important as physical skill.
- ▼ There have been great women role models in the game—from Babe Didrikson Zaharias and Patty Berg to Nancy Lopez.

With such prominent women golfers as Supreme Court Justice Sandra Day O'Connor, newspaper CEO Cathy Black, First Lady Hillary Clinton, New Jersey Governor Christine Todd Whitman and television personality Paula

Zahn, one would think the golf industry would welcome these demographically desirable golf enthusiasts with open arms.

Well, some have and some have not.

THE GOOD, THE BAD AND THE UGLY

Savvy marketing executives at premier companies such as Gillette, Chase Manhattan Bank, American Airlines and Cadillac have paid attention to the economic power of women golfers and have targeted them directly with promotional campaigns linked to golf by sponsoring golf clinics, advertising in *Golf For Women* and raising money for breast cancer research through golf events.

Yet the sad fact exists that when even the most powerful women attempt to play at some golf courses, they are treated as second-class citizens—or, in some cases, are barred totally.

A lawyer friend once described his disappointing experience when he accompanied a male and two female companions to a private golf course with public access. While the male paid the greens fees for the foursome, the women carried their clubs to the tee. Upon seeing the women, the owner grabbed some money out of the cash register and slammed it on the counter and yelled, "This isn't a playground! Get out!"

Journalist Marcia Chambers noted in her book, *The Unplayable Lie,* how the male privilege is embedded in club rules, bylaws and practices—a residue of the time when men had a virtual monopoly on institutional power and women were systematically excluded.

Some clubs do not allow women as members or guests

at all. Chambers also found clubs where women could be members but could not:

- ▼ Hold an equity interest.
- ▼ Vote.
- ▼ Sit on the board.
- ▼ Be single.
- ▼ Be divorced.
- ▼ Use certain facilities—such as the men's grille.
- ▼ Play golf on weekend mornings.

The issue of restricted tee times often infuriates businesswomen. These women work during the week—just as do their male counterparts. The rationale behind the policy—so say the clubs that hold women players to restricted tee times—is that women players are too slow. There are few men who can hit as quickly and as far as Jane.

A woman accountant and golfer tells a story about a client who invited her to play at his club. She was chagrined when she showed up promptly for tee time at 10 a.m. only to witness the pro in charge telling her friend very firmly that under no circumstances could they tee off until 1 p.m.!

If you want to know whether or not a club discriminates, the moral goes, it's not enough to ask if it has women members.

LADY SINGS THE BLUES

The issue of the grass ceiling is an emotional one for both sides. Women believe that restrictions on membership, tee times, and even access to the lounge for a post-round soda are simply unfair and unjust in a world in which gender-based barriers have all but been eliminated. Golf clubs are settings in which leaders of the business community, the bar, government and every other major industry and organization now gather. Women are full members of those economic arenas and should be welcome in the same places their male peers are welcome.

The governing bodies of many such clubs, however, hold to their constitutional right of private association. If they do not want to associate or admit women—or Blacks or Jews, or anyone else—as members they don't have to.

The number of such clubs is dwindling, however. The California Supreme Court recently ruled that a club is no longer truly private if it allows non-members to take lessons, shop at the pro shop or use club facilities for a fee—a legal standard other courts most likely will adopt.

This book will not solve the issue of the grass ceiling. As more businesswomen play golf with one another and with their male business peers, however, more pressure will be exerted on remnants of the old system that choose to exclude or curtail women's access to the green.

Until the new brigade of businesswomen golfers is large enough to change the customs that keep them out, all business executives—men and women—can do their part to eradicate the grass ceiling by refusing to:

- ✔ Play at or join clubs that discriminate.
- ✔ Sponsor tournaments at clubs that discriminate.
- ✔ Accept social invitations to clubs that discriminate.
- ✔ Subsidize club memberships for executives at clubs that discriminate.
- ✔ Allow their civic or business organizations to meet at clubs that discriminate.

- ✔ Arrange company outings at clubs that discriminate.
- ✔ Defend the conduct of clubs that discriminate.

TIP

As golf professional Tom Watson said, 'Let's discriminate right now, each one of us, privately, between what is right and what is wrong. At work, at the country club and at home with the children, let's make personal choices that help rather than hurt.'

SEVENTEEN

THE SEVEN MYTHS OF ETHICS

Few books or videos about golf include a discussion of ethics. Yet just as businesspeople are confronted with competing and often incompatible demands in the business world, so are golfers in the world of golf.

Some golfers think that ethics has no place on the golf course—adhering to several persistent stereotypes and myths about ethics. If you want to mix golf and business, you have to explode the following common myths regarding ethics:

1. Business ethics is an oxymoron . . . and so is golf ethics.

Several similarities about business and golf give rise to this myth. Golf is competitive, like business. Golf is individualistic, like business. Despite the popularity of the word "teamwork," the bottom line is that everyone is looking out for themselves. Whereas golf is about winning—beating the course or last week's score, business is about making more profits than last year or getting more market share than a competitor.

But just as the world of business is a world of complex human relationships—among manufacturers, retailers, vendors, investors, customers, bankers, analysts, service providers, regulators, community leaders and elected officials—golf is a strategic business tool in forming personal relationships. The best relationships are built on trust, and ethical behavior fosters trust. Golf and ethics, then, are fundamentally intertwined.

2. Ethics is a side issue, irrelevant to how one plays the game.

How one plays golf is the central issue of the game. Golf is a game of rules—but is played by individuals. Golf can't be ethical unless the individuals playing it operate in the context of a game that has shared values. The moral signposts of the game are:

- ✔ Character
- ✔ Honesty
- ✔ Trust
- ✔ Fairness
- ✔ Courtesy
- ✔ Structure

Individual players have a responsibility to uphold the tradition and culture of the game by playing ethically. Knowing the etiquette, standards of conduct and rules of the game is integral to upholding the game's ethical culture. Businesspeople cannot play golf successfully without behaving ethically on and off the course.

3. Ethics is the same as following the rules.

Indeed there are certain absolute principles of golf that must be obeyed, yet there are always situations in which a desirable end justifies a rule-breaking means. It is in balancing the two that the "ethics of care and concern" comes in. For example, a player must not move the ball—that's a rule. Yet if she has taken an excessive amount of strokes on a hole in a friendly game, she should pick up her ball and move along to the next hole so that she does not delay others.

Following the rules can be the minimum standard of behavior, but an ethical standard often requires additional consideration. Finally there are such things as unethical rules and laws. Anti-apartheid activists and any woman who has been shooed off a golf course can avow to that truism.

4. Ethics is a personal matter and has no role on the golf course.

There's a difference between a player's character and his or her actions. It is a person's character that is reflected in his or her respect for others and sense of responsibility to the game and to other players. A player might play by the literal rules and yet reveal his true character by inflating his handicap and then rationalize his dishonesty by saying, "I never get my share of tee times, good equipment or competent instructors." He might even insist on hitting first, calling it his right. This kind of player is focused solely on what he can get out of the game rather than on what he brings to it.

Businesspeople who play golf have an obligation to bring their sense of personal ethics to the game. They should always try to set an example of good behavior—action generated by good character.

5. Golf is not a truly competitive sport—no one is hurt if I try to improve my score however I can.

It may come as a surprise to players who have taken up golf with a real passion, but the mission of the game is to strive for excellence—not to win for personal gain. While it is true that golfers play their own individual ball and record an individual score, there are many instances in which teamwork, cooperation and respect for others of lower ability are required—particularly in business-sponsored golf events. A player who wants his personal expectations fulfilled at any cost does not understand the game and has no business being on the golf course.

6. Golf and ethics shouldn't mix—players should be able to enjoy the game without sermons.

Ethics is particularly well placed on the golf course because golf is usually played without referees, umpires or linesmen. Golf is regulated and officiated by the players themselves. Just as individuals do not suspend their sense of ethics while they're at work, they must not suspend them on the course.

7. There are no ethical absolutes—proper behavior is a matter of personal opinion.

It's tempting to think that moral judgments are expressions of personal preference, particularly on the golf course where it is not uncommon for one player to suggest to another, "You might try doing this or that." The player who has just been "coached" could in turn say, "Mind your own business"—after all, what could his companion do, turn him in to the club police at the end of the round? Not likely.

But in fact there is consensus about what constitutes ethical behavior on the golf course. Those in doubt should ask the experts—just as they would in the business world. If an expert isn't available or if he or she has trouble recognizing an action as ethical or unethical, you might put it to the following litmus test:

- ▼ Would I do it if I were playing with my boss?
- ▼ Would it be sportsmanlike if everyone else did it?
- ▼ If someone I respect asked me for advice about this what would I say?
- ▼ What alternatives do I have?
- ▼ Is it right?
- ▼ Is it fair?
- ▼ How would I like to see this described in the newspaper?
- ▼ What are my fundamental values?
- ▼ What ethical principles apply here?

The ideal ethical standard in golf is one that promotes utilitarianism, respect for the rights of others, sportsmanship and demonstrates concern for the environment, other players and the traditions of the game.

Just as business has a role in society beyond increasing profits, golfers, too, have a responsibility to the game that goes beyond carding low scores. A virtuous character not only directs an individual's actions, it inspires the actions of others well as.

TIP

Success in golf—like success in business—requires people with character and integrity.

EIGHTEEN

A WORD TO NONGOLFERS

You're the comptroller of a company and you've just approved an expenditure for two company executives to enter a local charity golf tournament and invite two clients.

You're the new head of sales and marketing for a national financial services firm and you've received a proposal inviting your company to be a participating sponsor at a local golf clinic and tournament.

Your wife is on the cusp of becoming a partner at the largest law firm in town and she's out playing golf for the third consecutive Saturday morning. You don't play golf.

We understand that nongolfers may not fully appreciate the changing dynamics of the game, particularly in the business world. We also understand that not all individuals want to learn to play golf—and that's okay. But we do suggest that business executives who want to keep current try to understand that golf is no longer just a sport—it has become quite an effective business tool. You don't have to play the game to understand its power.

Those who play golf usually have intense enthusiasm for the sport and generally enjoy sharing their love of the game in their conversations with other golf admirers. If you watch golf on television, can talk about golf or golfers or admire an executive's golf artifacts on his desk, you are demonstrating your respect for an activity that he holds dear. By simply engaging him in conversation about his passion you will be a step closer to establishing a personal tie that will help your business relationship.

TO DIE FOR

You no doubt already realize the marketing power of golf and the sponsorship opportunities it affords through televised tournaments and spectator events. The most sophisticated marketing companies in the world have become advocates of golf sponsorship because of the great demographic profile of the audience that golf events reach. It also is a game that generates intense loyalty among its audience.

You also have to admire golf for its reputation for credibility and excellence—attributes that have become unique in the sporting world. In an arena fraught with player strikes, allegations of tanking, unprofessional and unsportsmanlike behavior, golf has sustained its posture as the sport of moral superiority.

Although you don't participate in the game directly, there's no reason you can't enjoy the game vicariously and by doing so, have more in common with your business associates who are already true golf aficionados. Here are some ways to get closer to what's rapidly becoming the favorite pastime of the business world:

▼ Follow golf in newspapers and in golf magazines.

▼ Watch golf tournaments on television.

▼ Attend golf events.

- ▼ Volunteer at local tournaments.
- ▼ Sponsor golf clinics and tournaments.
- ▼ Select a new young golfer to follow on the professional tour.
- ▼ Understand the buying power and influence of golf enthusiasts.
- ▼ Buy golf memorabilia or books for friends and associates who play.

TIP

Don't let the phenomenon of America's favorite pastime pass you by.

Glossary

We all want to be able to talk the talk of golf when we're out on the course and not take instant offense when we overhear someone using the words "fat," "gross" or "thin" within our earshot. Too, we shouldn't have to wander aimlessly looking for the "19th hole" or look to the treetops when someone yells "birdie." So here is every term you'll ever hear on the course and every one you'll need to know to get going—and a few more besides.

Best ball, n. A competition in which each team of four records the best score shot on each hole.

Birdie, n. A score of one under par for the hole. If par is 4, and you shoot 3, that's a birdie.

Bite, n. Quick stopping action of a ball on the green. "That ball really took a bite."

Bogey, n. A score of one shot over par for the hole. If par is 4 and you shoot 5, that's a bogey.

Bunker, n. A prepared area of ground filled with sand. "Oh no, my ball went in the bunker."

Card, v. To obtain a score. She carded a 4.

Divot, n. The clump of grass or turf that comes up when you swing the club. It should be replaced.

Double par, n. A score of twice par for the hole—what Dawn-Marie shoots. At that point, you pick the ball up and go to the next tee.

Eagle, n. A score of two under par for the hole. Now you're getting the idea—2 on a par 4 hole.

Executive course, n. This is not just a course reserved for executives. Generally it is shorter, therefore faster, than traditional golf courses. The description probably derives from the assumption that executives can steal only a couple of hours away from the office. It also could be known as the busy mother course.

Fat, adj. Striking the ground with your club before you hit the ball. A fat shot usually takes a lot of turf with it.

Fore, n. A cry of warning issued when it appears that a struck ball could be a danger to an individual. It's the same as "oh no!" or "look out!" and the reason why you don't start to hit your ball until the party in front of you is well in the distance.

Gimme, n. Your opponent concedes a putt. The stroke must still be counted even though it is not executed. Gimmies are given when even you could not possibly miss a putt.

Gross, n. The actual number of strokes taken in a round. That's right, add up all the holes.

Ground your club, v. To touch the ground with your club. If you do this within a hazard it's a penalty.

Handicap, n. and v. An equalizing system which allows players of varying skill levels to compete with each other. This is why golf is so much better for business relationships than, say, tennis.

Hazard, n. An area filled with sand or water. As in, "This course is filled with hazards in addition to my lack of ability."

Honor, n. The right to tee off or play first by virtue of the fact that you had the lowest score on the previous hole. See "ready golf."

Hook, n. For a right-handed player, a ball that curves from right to left. "Your ball is missing the fairway because you have a wicked hook."

Index, n. A number indicative of a player's skill level. It's used to compute the player's handicap on a specific course. If your index is 10 and the par for the course is 72, your handicap is 82.

Lie, n. or v. Position of the ball on the ground. Also what some golfers are known to do about their score.

Long irons, n. The 1, 2, 3 and 4 irons.

Low ball/low total, n. A competition in which one point is awarded on each hole for the lowest individual score and one point for the lowest team score.

Marker, n. An object used to identify the precise location of the ball on a putting green. If you were to replace your ball with a penny, that is your marker.

Mulligan, n. A shot you can take over in friendly matches only. Agree on how many mulligans you'll allow before you start the round. Usually taken on the first hole but not allowed under golf rules.

Nassau, n. A bet or wager comprised of three parts: the winning total on the front nine holes, the winning total on the back nine holes and the winning total score.

Par, n. The regulation number of strokes that are set for a particular hole from tee to cup if played flawlessly. The par for each hole will be listed on the course scorecard you pick up when you start to play.

90-degree rule, n. The rule that indicates carts may only enter and exit fairways on a 90-degree angle.

19th hole, n. An idiom for a place to convene—usually for drinks, after playing a round of golf.

Pitch and putt course, n. A short course—generally nine holes with par 27. Shorter than an executive (or busy mother) course.

Ready golf, n. The practice of allowing the first player who gets to his ball the right to hit first. This speeds up the game by saving time.

Rough, n. The part of the course that is left after you deduct the fairway, the green, the tee and all hazards. It is the edge of the course generally bordered by tall grass, trees, houses and other materials that will make your ball an unplayable lie.

Sand, adj. A description to go along with "Oh no!," usually attached to trap or bunker.

Scotch foursome, n. A competition format in which every team member plays the same ball, alternating shots.

Scramble, n. A competition in which the team chooses the best shot as the ball in play on each hole.

Scratch, n. or adj. An even par score. A scratch golfer has zero handicap. Jane is better than a scratch golfer.

Shotgun start, n. A competition format in which the teams start playing from various holes rather than all teams beginning at the first hole.

Skin, n. A hole-by-hole wagering system in which the lowest score on each hole wins. If there is a tie the amount of money wagered rolls over until someone wins a hole outright.

Shank, n. The dreaded shot that is improperly struck on the inside of the club face and causes the ball to veer to the right.

Short game, n. The portion of the game that begins about 100 yards from the hole.

Short irons, n. The 7, 8 and 9 irons, pitching wedge and sand wedge.

Slice, n. For a right-handed player, a ball that curves from left to right. "Your ball is missing the fairway because you have a wicked slice."

Stroke play, n. A competition in which the total number of strokes hit determines the winner.

Thin, adj. When the club strikes only the top portion of the ball causing lower than desired trajectory. "Your swing is a little thin and that's why the ball just dribbles three feet in front of you."

Trajectory, n. The flight pattern of the ball. Jane's trajectory is up, up and away!

Unplayable lie, n. A ball has landed in a position that makes it impossible to hit—such as when it lands under a lounge chair. The player makes the determination of an unplayable lie.

Whiff, n. A swing that completely misses the ball but must be counted toward your score. It may seem unfair to count whiffs but even pros have been known to miss the ball.

About The Authors

After taking up golf when she was 13, Jane Blalock hasn't stopped since. A professional golfer for 18 years on the Ladies Professional Golf Association tour, Blalock has won 29 titles, two Triple Crown titles and three World Ladies Championships in Japan. The seventh professional on the women's tour to achieve $1 million in career earnings, Blalock still holds the record of playing 299 tournaments without missing a cut.

As president of The Jane Blalock Company, Blalock now organizes golf and tennis clinics, as well as tournaments and events for corporate clients—including the distinguished Gillette LPGA Golf Clinics for women, the Cadillac Golf Series and the Volvo Legend Series. She also is a color analyst for ESPN and Prime Sports golf events.

Dawn-Marie Driscoll is a businesswoman who has been honored for her research and writing about business leadership and career development. Formerly vice president of corporate affairs and general counsel of Filene's, a Boston-based department store chain, and a law partner at Palmer & Dodge, currently she is a director of several mutual funds and private companies. Co-author of *Members of the Club: The Coming of Age of Executive Women* and *The Ethical Edge: Tales of Organizations That Have Faced Moral Crises,* she is a beginning golfer who gladly welcomes any free strokes.

Both authors speak frequently about issues concerning building personal relationships, social values and how golf can be used as a an effective tool in rainmaking and business development as well as about marketing issues relevant to a rapidly growing audience of influential golf participants.

The authors are available as key-note speakers. Please contact MasterMedia's Speakers' Bureau for availability and fee arrangements. Call Tony Colao at 908-359-1612 or fax 908-359-1647.

MasterMedia Limited

To order copies of *Gimmies, Bogeys and Business: An Insider's Guide On How To Use Golf For Professional Success,* call or write:

MasterMedia Limited
17 East 89th Street
New York, NY 10128
(212) 546-7650
(800) 334-8232
(212) 546-8179 (fax)

(Please use MasterCard or VISA on phone orders)

An Invitation

If you found this book helpful and want to receive a MasterMedia book catalog or newsletter that contains a list of MasterMedia's inspirational books that carry the Heritage Imprint, write or fax to the above address or phone number.

MasterMedia is the only company to combine publishing with a full-service Speakers' Bureau.

MasterMedia books and speakers cover today's important issues—from family values to health topics and business ethics.

For information and a complete list of speakers, call (800) 453-2887 or fax (908) 359-1647.

Other MasterMedia Books

To order additional copies of any MasterMedia book, send a check for the price of the book plus $2.00 postage and handling for the first book, $1.00 for each additional book to:

MasterMedia Limited
17 East 89th Street
New York, NY 10128
(212) 546-7650
(800) 334-8232
(212) 546-8179 (fax)

(Please use Master Card or Visa on phone orders)

AGING PARENTS AND YOU: A Complete Handbook to Help You Help Your Elders Maintain a Healthy, Productive and Independent Life, by Eugenia Anderson-Ellis, is a complete guide to providing care to aging relatives. It gives practical advice and resources to the adults who are helping their elders lead productive and independent lives. Revised and updated. ($9.95 paper)

BALANCING ACTS! Juggling Love, Work, Family and Recreation, by Susan Schiffer Stautberg and Marcia Worthing, provides strategies to lead a balanced life by reordering priorities and setting realistic goals. ($12.95 paper)

BEATING THE AGE GAME: Redefining Retirement, by Jack and Phoebe Ballard, debunks the myth that retirement means sitting out the rest of the game. The years between 55 and 80 can be your best, says the authors, who provide ample examples of people successfully using retirement to reinvent their lives. ($12.95 paper)

THE BIG APPLE BUSINESS AND PLEASURE GUIDE: 501 Ways to Work Smarter, Play Harder, and Live Better in New York City, by Muriel Siebert and Susan Kleinman, offers visitors and New Yorkers alike advice on how to do business in the city and enjoy its attractions. ($9.95 paper)

BREATHING SPACE: Living and Working at a Comfortable Pace in a Sped-Up Society, by Jeff Davidson, helps readers handle information and activity overload and gain greater control over their lives. ($10.95 paper)

CARVING WOOD AND STONE, by Arnold Prince, is an illustrated step-by-step handbook demonstrating all you need to hone your wood and carving skills. ($15.95 paper)

THE COLLEGE COOKBOOK II, For Students by Students, by Nancy Levicki, is a handy volume of recipes culled from college students across the U.S. ($11.95 paper)

THE CONFIDENCE FACTOR: How Self-Esteem Can Change Your Life, by Dr. Judith Briles, is based on a nationwide survey of 6,000 men and women. Briles explores why women often feel a lack of self-confidence and have a poor opinion of themselves. She offers step-by-step advice on becoming the person you want to be. ($12.95 paper, $18.95 cloth)

CUPID, COUPLES & CONTRACTS: A Guide to Living Together, Prenuptial Agreements, and Divorce, by Lester Wallman, with Sharon McDonnell, is an insightful, consumer-oriented handbook that provides a comprehensive overview of family law, including prenuptial agreements, alimony and fathers' rights. ($12.95 paper)

THE DOLLARS AND SENSE OF DIVORCE: The Financial Guide for Women, by Dr. Judith Briles, is the first book to combine the legal hurdles by planning finances before, during and after divorce. ($10.95 paper)

FINANCIAL SAVVY FOR WOMEN: A Money Book for Women of All Ages, by Dr. Judith Briles, divides a woman's monetary lifespan into six phases, discusses specific issues to be addressed at each stage and demonstrates how to create a sound money plan. ($15.00 paper)

FLIGHT PLAN FOR LIVING: The Art of Self-Encouragement, by Patrick O'Dooley, is a guide organized like a pilot's checklist, to ensure you'll be flying "clear to the top" throughout your life. ($17.95 cloth)

HOT HEALTH-CARE CAREERS, by Margaret McNally and Phyllis Schneider, offers readers what they need to know about training for and getting jobs in a field where professionals are always in demand. ($10.95 paper)

HOW NOT TO GET FIRED: Ten Steps to Becoming an Indispensable Employee, by Carole Hyatt, shows readers how to take a fresh look at their career paths, adapt to the current marketplace by using old skills in new way and discover options they didn't know they had. ($12.95 paper)

HOW TO GET WHAT YOU WANT FROM ALMOST ANYBODY, by T. Scott Gross, shows how to get great service, negotiate better prices and always get what you pay for. ($9.95 paper)

KIDS WHO MAKE A DIFFERENCE, by Joyce Roché and Marie Rodriguez, is an inspiring document on how today's toughest challenges are being met by teenagers and kids, whose courage and creativity enables them to find practical solutions! ($8.95 paper, with photos)

LEADING YOUR POSITIVELY OUTRAGEOUS SERVICE TEAM, by T. Scott Gross, forgoes theory in favor of a hands-on approach, Gross providing a step-by-step formula for developing self-managing service teams that put the customer first. ($12.95 paper)

LIFE'S THIRD ACT: Taking Control of Your Mature Years, by Patricia Burnham, Ph.D., is a perceptive handbook for everyone who recognizes that planning is the key to enjoying your mature years. ($10.95 paper, $18.95 cloth)

LISTEN TO WIN: A Guide to Effective Listening, by Curt Bechler and Richard Weaver, Ph.D.s, is a powerful, people-oriented book that will help you learn to live with others, connect with them and get the best from them. ($18.95 cloth)

THE LIVING HEART BRAND NAME SHOPPER'S GUIDE, (3d edition), by Michael DeBakey, M.D., Antonio Gotto, Jr., M.D., Lynne Scott, M.A., R.D./L.D., and John Foreyt, Ph.D., lists brand name products low in fat, saturated fatty acids and cholesterol. (14.95 paper)

THE LIVING HEART GUIDE TO EATING OUT, by Michael DeBakey, Antonio Gotto, Jr., Lynne Scott, is an essential handbook for people who want to maintain a health-conscious diet when dining in all types of restaurants. ($9.95 paper)

MAKING YOUR DREAMS COME TRUE NOW!, by Marcia Wieder, introduces an easy, unique, and practical technique for defining, pursuing, and realizing your career and life interests. Filled with stories of real people and helpful exercises, plus a personal workbook. (Revised and updated, $10.95 paper)

MANAGING IT ALL: Time-Saving Ideas for Career, Family, Relationships, and Self, by Beverly Benz Treuille and Susan Schiffer Stautberg, is written for women who are juggling careers and families. More than 200 career women (ranging from a TV anchorwoman to an investment banker) were interviewed. The book contains many humorous anecdotes on saving time and improving the quality of life for self and family. ($9.95 paper)

MANAGING YOUR CHILD'S DIABETES, by Robert Wood Johnson IV, Sale Johnson, Casey Johnson, and Susan Kleinman, brings help to families trying to understand diabetes and control its effects. ($10.95 paper)

MANAGING YOUR PSORIASIS, by Nicholas J. Lowe, M.D., is an innovative manual that couples scientific research and encouraging support, with an emphasis on how patients can take charge of their health. ($10.95 paper, $17.95 cloth)

MANN FOR ALL SEASONS: Wit and Wisdom from The Wahington Post's Judy Mann, shows the columnist at her best as she writes about women, families and the impact and politics of the women's revolution. ($9.95 paper, $19.95 cloth)

MIND YOUR OWN BUSINESS: And Keep it in the Family, by Marcy Syms, CEO of Syms Corp., is an effective guide for any organization facing the toughest step in managing a family business—making the transition to the new generation. ($12.95 paper, $18.95 cloth)

OFFICE BIOLOGY: Why Tuesday is the Most Productive Day and Other Relevant Facts for Survival in the Workplace, by Edith Weiner and Arnold Brown, teaches how in the '90s and beyond we will be expected to work smarter, take better control of our health, adapt to advancing technology and improve our lives in ways that are not too costly or resource-intensive. ($12.95 paper, $21.95 cloth)

ON TARGET: Enhance Your Life and Advance Your Career, by Jeri Sedlar and Rick Miners, is a neatly woven tapestry of insights on career and life issues gathered from audiences across the country. This feedback has been crystallized into a highly readable guide for exploring what you want. ($11.95 paper)

PAIN RELIEF: How to Say No to Acute, Chronic, and Cancer Pain!, by Dr. Jane Cowles, offers a step-by-step plan for assessing pain and communicating it to your doctor, and explains the importance of having a pain plan before undergoing any medical or surgical treatment. Includes "The Pain Patient's Bill of Rights," and a reusable pain assessment chart. ($14.95 paper, $22.95 cloth)

POSITIVELY OUTRAGEOUS SERVICE: New and Easy Ways to Win Customers for Life, by T. Scott Gross, identifies what '90s consumers really want and how business can develop effective marketing strategies to answer those needs. ($14.95 paper)

THE PREGNANCY AND MOTHERHOOD DIARY: Planning the First Year of Your Second Career, by Susan Schiffer Stautberg, is the first and only undated appointment diary that shows how to manage pregnancy and career. ($12.95 spiral bound)

REAL BEAUTY...REAL WOMEN: A Handbook for Making the Best of Your Own Good Looks, by Kathleen Walas, international beauty and fashion director of Avon Products, Inc., offers expert advice on beauty and fashion for women of all ages and ethnic backgrounds. A Heritage Imprint book. ($19.50 paper)

ROSEY GRIER'S ALL-AMERICAN HEROES: Multicultural Success Stories, by Roosevelt "Rosey" Grier, is a candid collection of profiles of prominent African Americans, Latins, Asians, and Native Americans who reveal how they achieved public acclaim and personal success. ($9.95 paper, with photos)

A SEAT AT THE TABLE: An Insider's Guide for America's New Women Leaders, by Patricia Harrison. A must-read guide that offers practical advice for women who want to serve on boards of directors, play key roles in politics and community affairs or become policy makers in public or private sectors. ($19.95 cloth)

SELLING YOURSELF: Be the Competent, Confident Person You Really Are!, by Kathy Thebo, Joyce Newman, and Diana Lynn. The ability to express yourself effectively and to project a confident image is essential in today's fast-paced world where professional and personal lines frequently cross. ($12.95 paper)

SHOCKWAVES: The Global Impact of Sexual Harassment, by Susan L. Webb, examines the problem of sexual harassment today in every kind of workplace around the world. Well-researched, this manual provides the most recent information available, including legal changes in progress. ($11.95 paper, $19.95 cloth)

SOMEONE ELSE'S SON, by Alan Winter, explores the parent-child bond in a contemporary novel of lost identities, family secrets and relationships gone awry. Eighteen years after bringing their first son home from the hospital, Tish and Brad Hunter discover they are not his biological parents. ($18.95 cloth)

STEP FORWARD: Sexual Harassment in the Workplace, by Susan L. Webb, presents the facts for dealing with sexual harassment on the job. ($9.95 paper)

THE STEPPARENT CHALLENGE: A Primer for Making it Work, by Stephen Williams, Ph.D., offers insight into the many aspects of step relationships—from financial issues to lifestyle changes to differences in race or religion that affect the whole family. ($13.95 paper)

STRAIGHT TALK ON WOMEN'S HEALTH: How to Get the Health Care You Deserve, by Janice Teal, Ph.D., and Phyllis Schneider, is destined to become a health-care "bible." Devoid of confusing medical jargon, it offers a wealth of resources, including contact lists of health lines and women's medical centers. ($14.95 paper)

TEAMBUILT: Making Teamwork Work, by Mark Sanborn, teaches businesses how to increase productivity, without increasing resources or expenses, by building teamwork among employees. ($12.95 paper, $19.95 cloth)

A TEEN'S GUIDE TO BUSINESS: The Secrets to a Successful Enterprise, by Linda Menzies, Oren Jenkins, and Rick Fisher, provides solid information about starting your own business or working for one. ($7.95 paper)

WHAT KIDS LIKE TO DO, by Edward Stautberg, Gail Wubbenhorst, Atiya Easterling, and Phyllis Schneider, is a handy guide for parents, grandparents, and baby sitters. Written by kids for kind, this is an easy-to-read, generously illustrated primer for teaching families how to make every day more fun. ($7.95 paper)

WHEN THE WRONG THING IS RIGHT: How to Overcome Conventional Wisdom, Popular Opinion, and All the Lies Your Parents Told You, by Sylvia Bigelson, Ed.S., and Virginia McCullough, addresses issues such as marriage, relationships, parents and siblings, divorce, sex, money and careers, and encourages readers to break free from the pressures of common wisdom and to trust their own choices. ($9.95 paper)

WHY MEN MARRY: Insights From Marrying Men, by A.T. Langford, interviews with 64 men revealing their views on marriage. These men describe what scares them about women, how potential partners are tested, and how it feels to be a "marriage object." ($18.95 cloth)

A WOMAN'S PLACE IS EVERYWHERE: Inspirational Profiles of Female Leaders Who are Expanding the Roles of American Women, by Lindsey Johnson and Jackie Joyner-Kersee, profiles 30 women whose personal and professional achievements are helping to shape and expand our ideas of what's possible for humankind. ($9.95 paper)

THE WORKING MOM ON THE RUN MANUAL: by Debbie Nigro, is a humorous practical guide for working parents, particularly single, working Moms. Offers insights about careers, disciplining the kids, coping with husbands who won't do housework, running a home-based business and keeping track of just about everything every day. ($9.95 paper)

YOUR VISION: All About Modern Eye Care, by Warren D. Cross Jr., M.D., and Lawrence Lynn, Ph.D., reveals astounding research discoveries in an entertaining and informative handbook written with the patient in mind. ($13.95 paper)

WORLD RIDE: Going The Extra Mile Against Cancer, by Richard Drorbaugh, is a fast-paced, high-spirited, humorous and passionate narrative that dramatizes the mission—a 32-country bike tour—the author and his two teammates undertook to bring global attention to a universal disease. ($11.95 paper)

THE HERITAGE IMPRINT OF INSPIRATIONAL BOOKS

MasterMedia's Heritage Imprint books speak of courage, integrity and bouncing back from defeat. For the millions of Americans seeking greater purpose and meaning in their lives in difficult times, here are volumes of inspiration, solace and spiritual support.

The Heritage Imprint books are supported by MasterMedia's full-service Speakers' Bureau, authors' media and lecture tours, syndicated radio interviews, national and co-op advertising and publicity.

AMERICAN HEROES: Their Lives, Their Values, Their Beliefs, by Dr. Robert B. Pamplin, Jr., with Gary Eisler. Courage. Integrity. Compassion. The qualities of the hero still live in American men and women today—even in a world that is filled with disillusionment. Share their stories of outstanding achievements, and discover the values that guide their lives as revealed in a pioneering coast-to-coast survey. ($18.95 cloth)

THE ETHICAL EDGE: Tales of Organizations That Have Faced Moral Crises, by Dawn-Marie Driscoll, W. Michael Hoffman, Edward S. Petry, associated with The Center for Business Ethics at Bentley College. The authors link the current search for meaning and values in life with stories of corporate turnarounds. Now read about organizations that have recovered from moral crises—the tough lessons they've learned, ethical structures they've put in place to ensure a solid future. If every employee followed the mission of the book, America's companies would clearly have not only a moral edge, but a compctitive edge as well. ($24.95 cloth)

HERITAGE: The Making of the American Family, by Robert Pamplin Jr., Gary Eisler, Jeff Sengstack, and John Domini, mixes history and philosophy in a biographical saga of the Pamplins' phenomenal ascent to wealth and the creation of one of the largest private fortunes in the U.S. ($24.95 cloth)

JOURNEY TOWARD FORGIVENESS: Finding Your Way Home, by BettyClare Moffatt, is a delightfully positive inspirational self-help book that provides spiritual guidelines to forgiveness, meditation, prayer, action, healing and change. ($11.95 paper)

PRELUDE TO SURRENDER: The Pamplin Family and The Siege of Petersburg, by Robert B. Pamplin, Jr., with Gary Eisler, Jeff Sengstack and John Domini. Engaging account of how the author's ancestral home was taken over by the Confederacy for use as a hospital and as a defensive position. It is now the Pamplin Park Civil War Site. ($10.95 paper)

RESILIENCY: How to Bounce Back Faster, Stronger, Smarter, by Tessa Albert Warschaw, Ph.D. and Dee Barlow, Ph.D). Packed with practical techniques and insights on solving old problems in new ways, the book also shows readers how to become more resilient in their personal and professional lives and teaches the skills for bouncing back from everyday stresses to surviving disastrous multiple losses. You will learn to enthusiastically embrace life. ($21.95 cloth)